THE CROSSINGS

INSPIRED BY TRUE EVENTS

J.E. KROSS & D.J. MILNE

Rowe Publishing

ISBN: 978-1-939054-94-4 (softcover)
ISBN: 978-1-939054-95-1 (hardcover)

Cover design: Pixel Experiment
Cover photo: Dairo Chamorro

1 3 5 7 9 8 6 4 2

Printed in the United States of America
Published by

Rowe Publishing

www.rowepub.com

For Katherine

Who fearlessly paved the way
for future females on the railroad.

You are loved and you are missed.
May you forever rest in peace.

ACKNOWLEDGMENTS

The authors would like to say thank you to the following people for their help, love, and support during this adventure:

- ~ The family of D. J. Milne: James, Elizabeth, Colleen, Andrea, James Stephen, Norm and Dolores
- ~ Gary (Wilberta), Michele (Barry), Nancy (Chuck), Doug (Lisa), David (Laurie)
- ~ The family of J. E. Kross: Joseph, Lauren, and Joey
- ~ Jean and Norm Preston, Alan Boetticher, James Bonner, Jeff Medor, and Thea Whitcomb
- ~ Barry Kerch for finding time in his busy schedule to read and be so supportive.
- ~ C.C., for being my biggest fan.
- ~ Our railroad family: our brothers, sisters, and managers who enthusiastically read pieces, parts, and continually supported us
- ~ Julie Macdonald, Liz Conforti, Stacy Sweet, and Peggy Kordana
- ~ Dairo Chamorro, Philip Freeman of Kevin Anderson & Associates, and Miranda Spencer of Red Panda Communications
- ~ Sherri of Rowe Publishing. You rock!

CHAPTER I

Majick

Rutland, Vermont
December 13, 2016, 11:33 PM

Claire paused at the edge of the forest. Her black satin robe billowed behind her as she sniffed the air suspiciously.

The darkened woods awaited her. She threw a glance over her shoulder before continuing on. She carried a broom under one arm, and an aging altar that concealed some of her tools under the other.

She pulled her hood lower. The scar on her left cheek was barely visible, but she ran her fingertips along the gash as though making sure it was still there. It was still there. It had been there for over thirty years; it would always be there.

The crunch of her steel-toed black leather boots on the ice reverberated through the silent night. The sky was alive with tiny bursts of blue and white light. The waxing moon was almost full.

She had been waiting patiently for such a moon. Her green eyes began to shine as she looked up at it.

Claire continued across the snow and ice. As she passed the edge of the parking lot, she seemed to step from light into darkness. The frigid air had already penetrated her black leather gloves, pricking her pale fingers like a thousand needles.

Guided only by moonlight, she continued through the congregation of trees. She passed a cluster of tall green pines and blue spruces, and there it was—the Sun Wheel.

An astronomy professor had designed the Sun Wheel in the 1940s, to mark solar trajectory. It was a cross, situated within a large circle, with grayish-white boulders marking the four compass points. Other boulders indicated various important events like the solstices and equinoxes.

Claire strode into the center of the wheel and placed her altar on one of the flat-topped boulders. She propped her wand and broom against a small drift of snow.

She untied the small knot at the base of her neck and removed her hood, and looked up to the sky. She was able to make out the fiery glow of Venus and knew that Jupiter, with its brilliant blue light, was out tonight too. The two planets she wanted to influence were aligned; it was the perfect time and place for the work that needed to be done.

The area was deserted. The Witching Hour was approaching quickly. It was time.

She undid the leather strap on the outside of the black Book of Shadows nestled within the ancient altar. Pulling out a handful of gravel, she placed it before the rock representing the North. The element of earth symbolized strength and stability. Working her way around the wheel clockwise, she stopped at each of the directional stones. At the East-facing stone, she set a candle—symbolizing fire and transformation—in a smooth crystal holder and lit it. At the South-facing stone, she jammed a large stick with bells attached to it—symbolizing air and communication—into the ground; they clanked in the cold breeze. At the West-facing stone, she placed a silver chalice and filled it with spring water from a vial, symbolizing water and emotion.

Her wand was created from a branch that had fallen from one of the mighty oak trees in the Salem, Massachusetts cemetery. She had spent many nights meticulously etching the symbols of the Ancient Ones into it. She had consecrated it before wrapping it in leather and copper tubing. Only the tip was whittled and left bare. A clear quartz stone was mounted just below the wand's handle.

She picked up the wand and returned to the North-facing stone, her left hand raised toward the sky. Walking in a clockwise motion in a trancelike state, she murmured a chant in a barely audible voice, just above a whisper. When her motions were complete, she placed the wand back on the altar and removed a five-pointed silver star from her altar box. She walked into the center of the circle and extended her arms toward the sky. She felt the wind pick up speed for just a moment, and then subside peacefully.

Claire lowered herself to the ground to complete the ritual, and again stretched her arms over her head. She used the candle positioned at the East-facing stone to light one corner of the piece of parchment paper that had been in her pocket. The words written upon it had been prepared with great care, in anticipation of this night. She watched in silence as the paper burned down to ash, which began its midnight flight to the cosmos to do her bidding.

"So mote it be," Claire said, almost to herself.

Claire rose to her feet, brushed some of the snow from her clothes, and placed the star back in the box. She picked up her wand from the altar and walked to the North-facing stone, raising her right arm above her head one more time.

"The circle may be undone but not broken," she chanted. "Merry meet, merry part, and merry meet again."

From the corner of her eye, Claire saw two brilliant spheres of light floating toward her and flinched. As the spheres drew closer, Claire could feel the presence of her mother and grandmother. Thoughts and images floated across her mind's eye like a screen, and she felt a sudden sense of urgency as they communicated with her.

She knew that the presence of the spheres was a direct result of her request for protection from the Ancient Ones. Still, she had flinched as they materialized from the darkness.

Lately, when Claire showed up at work, a trace scent would irritate her nostrils. She knew that smell; it told her that something ominous was about to happen. Sometimes she would catch a glimpse of a dark figure with red eyes lurking in the corners. Mom and Nana were now telling her to pay close attention to these signs.

Claire was struck by the way these messages were being presented to her. Normally, when she was shown future events or given information, the colors were vivid, unearthly, even dazzling. But these images were cloudy and dull. Most of them were too difficult to make out with any clarity. The parts she could perceive were dark and ominous. Railroad tracks in the dead of night. Feelings of dread.

Claire heard the sound of an animal screeching in pain, and whirled around in a circle, staring out into the blackness that surrounded her. She felt eyes on her, and shuddered, just as the harsh and unmistakable smell reached her nostrils. She nervously rubbed the scar that ran down the left side of her face. She knew what the smell was. It was burning hair and sulfur. It was hideous. It was *his* smell.

The images dissipated as quickly as they'd materialized, as Claire focused on the demonic red eyes that now peered at her from the darkened woods. The two spheres that had been circling her rose high into the sky and disappeared among the stars.

The malevolent eyes stared through the dead-seeming forest for a long moment, then twinkled briefly and disappeared into nothingness. A chill raced through Claire's body. She collected her tools and repacked the altar, and walked back through the woods. She no longer noticed the cold night air or the icy ground crunching under her feet. Her mind was consumed with a sense of impending danger.

As she emerged from the forest and crossed the otherwise empty parking lot, relief washed over her. Her car was in sight.

The drive home to St. Albans was a long one and it felt that much longer as she contemplated her aloneness, in life as well as in her craft. Still, she felt a sense of gratitude at having somehow been able to keep this part of her life private— even on the railroad, where everyone knew everyone else's business.

The only person who knew that she was a Witch was her friend Teri Cooper, and that was only because Teri had walked in on her in the ladies' locker room while she was "taking care of a problem"—an event they now referred to as the Cayenne Pepper Incident.

Claire was a brand-new locomotive engineer then. Getting there had been a tough enough venture on its own. Being female made it akin to being a seal in a shark tank. She'd been having a lot of problems with Adam, her road foreman (aka Great White). He was much harder on her than her male peers, constantly undermining her and double- and triple-checking her work, grinding away at her confidence. On that particular day, a friend had called to tip her off that he was going to be giving her a compliance ride... again.

Claire understood that a new engineer was monitored closely. But the constant compliance rides and equipment downloads (to see whether an engineer was speeding, or not blowing the horn properly at crossings, and so on) that Adam put her through bordered on harassment.

Claire remembered the cayenne pepper incident all too clearly. Arriving at work early, she had dashed from the parking lot through the crew base and into the ladies' locker room. She'd washed out the mason jar she'd purchased on the way in with a sneaky gleam in her eye.

Reaching into her bag, she'd retrieved half a sheet of parchment paper. Her intent was simple—to stop Adam's attacks. If done correctly, the charm would lob his attacks back onto himself threefold. She'd carefully written his full name on the paper and tucked it into the jar. Then she'd opened a bottle of cayenne pepper, also newly purchased, and begun to pour it in. It was only supposed to be a teaspoonful, but Teri had come bumbling in and startled her.

"What the hell are you doing?" Teri had demanded.

Claire had tried to ignore her and keep working, but her wrist had twitched, sending nearly half the bottle of pepper into the jar. She'd screwed the jar's lid on tight and shaken it. As the paper slid toward the bottom, Adam's name had been inundated with cayenne. Claire had known it was much too much spice, but there was no turning back.

"Don't worry. I'm just protecting myself from Adam," Claire had said, adding, "I'm your engineer today."

Teri was a conductor—a good one—and they'd be working together for the first time.

"I will explain it to you when we get to Albany," Claire said. She paused, then looked into the other woman's eyes. "Just leave it alone."

"No problem there," Teri replied sarcastically, suddenly finding something under her fingernail more interesting.

Claire had instantly known that Teri wouldn't share what she had witnessed. Not only because of her apparently limited attention span, but also because of the unwritten code that women on the railroad stuck together. Her secret would be safe, at least for the next few hours.

She recalled the job briefing later that day, a short meeting to go over speed restrictions, work zones, and the like. Teri had Tommy as her assistant conductor, and was commenting to him that it was strange how Adam hadn't joined them yet. In fact, he wasn't around the crew room at all. Teri kept glancing over at Claire suspiciously.

The station master's voice boomed over the intercom: "Track two, ladies and gentlemen. Your train is coming down from the maintenance facility as we speak."

Walking toward the arriving train on the departure tracks, Claire, Teri, and Tommy finally spotted Adam. He was headed toward his car in the employee parking lot, and moving like he didn't feel well at all.

Chuck, the other road foreman, clad in a white company hard hat and a "Canadian tuxedo"— denim jacket and blue jeans—crossed the three sets of tracks and came up the cement ramp toward the group.

"Claire," he called out, "I will be riding with you today to do your compliance check, even though I know Adam just gave you one." With a mildly annoyed air, he waved over Teri and Tommy for another briefing, as the crew had changed. The two conductors, who were further down the platform, saw Chuck waving and headed back.

When they were finished, Teri had asked Chuck why Adam wasn't going to be doing the evaluation. He told her that Adam had suddenly developed a fever and was very ill.

The ringing bell and roar of the diesel engine hadn't allowed for any more conversation between Claire and Teri, who stood on the platform staring at one another. Claire had given the other woman a wink, and then climbed up and disappeared inside the engine, with Chuck in tow. Teri shook her head uncomfortably, tipped her conductor's hat up over her bangs, and walked back toward her door in the coaches.

Claire pondered the memory as she parked her car in front of her condo and shut the engine off. The street was quiet. The evening's spell work was set in motion.

Thinking about that smell from the forest, and those eyes bearing down on her, made her shiver. She pulled the keys from the ignition and leaned back in the seat, gazing out at the snowcapped bushes that lined her sidewalk.

You have to be twice as good to be considered half as good. As a student engineer, she had heard that saying repeatedly, during class and from the handful of women across the country that had dared to encroach upon this male-dominated profession.

There had been some rough trips. She thought about the time a train had broken down in the middle of nowhere at 3:00 AM during a scorching August. She remembered being screamed at to fix the problem, while still trying to solve the problem, and trying not to succumb to heatstroke. Despite the suspicions of distrustful supervisors like Adam and some knuckle-walking co-workers, though, Claire's obvious knowledge and calm demeanor eventually earned her a reputation as a solid engineer.

She had held the job for a few years, and enjoyed the work, but she'd decided to apply for the position of road foreman. This would make her a supervisor, but she could still be called upon to run trains in the event of an emergency.

When she'd spotted the opening, she knew she had already met most of the requirements. Nevertheless, she put a little "elemental influence" to work right after submitting her application. In Claire's experience, employing Majick always seemed to work, but one needed to be very careful what one asked for, as well as how one asked, or things could get complicated.

Soon afterward, she had been offered the road foreman's position and begun supervising many of the same engineers with whom she had hired out on the railroad with. And as for Adam…well, he had transferred out of the area shortly afterward, with no explanation. There wasn't a day that went by that Claire missed him.

CHAPTER 2

The Train, the Witch and the Conductor

Muir's Mountain, St. Albans, Vermont
February 3, 2017, 4:00 PM

The airbrakes took hold with an unmistakable screech as the locomotive's wheels instantly began to grind against the rail. It was the sound of a train trying to stop itself, a moment after the panicked engineer had thrown the emergency brake handle into position.

A human figure, completely covered in dark blankets, had been standing motionless in the center of the tracks. Whoever it was had never even turned around to look as the train barreled toward it at 110 miles per hour. The brakes squealed, the horn blared, the bell rang, and then there was the inevitable *thud* of impact. The locomotive and the five coaches trailing behind it, approximately 1.4 million pounds of steel all together, had plowed into the solitary, silent human body like a wind-shield smacking a bug. A life ended, just like that.

Caleb, the engineer, veins flooded with pure adrenaline, immediately grabbed the radio microphone from the locomotive's control panel. "Emergency! Emergency! Emergency! Train number 34 in emergency at milepost 117, over," he blurted.

Hops and Vines Lounge,
Southern St. Albans, Vermont, 4:15 PM

"Happy hour," Claire whispered to herself, hearing Eddie Money's voice coming from the bar's half-open door as she stepped out of her red coupe and onto the sidewalk. She tugged her hair into place beside her cheek, trying to cover her scar. Before she could get inside, though, never mind order a drink, she felt an emptiness deep in her gut. Something had happened.

She pulled out her railroad-issued cell phone and looked at the screen. Nothing. Tucking it back in her coat pocket as she locked her car with the key fob, she glanced down the hill.

A portion of Lake Champlain was visible from where she stood. It was visible from pretty much anywhere one went in St. Albans; she loved that aspect of life in town. The lake was expansive and truly majestic, lined with towering pines and oaks holding their own under the snow and ice, with hawks floating effortlessly through the crisp air.

The lake allowed her to feel as if she were living inside of a painting. It provided a level of inspiration one simply couldn't get walking out of a bodega onto a people-cluttered Manhattan sidewalk. The landscape was littered with pickup trucks and ice shanties, though the fishermen weren't visible. *Maybe they were second-guessing their decision to be out there on such a cold day,* Claire thought. The odd thing was, if you looked just a half mile farther down the lake, it was open water.

She walked past the fluorescent green "Hops and Vines" sign that covered the side of the building, and entered the bar through the front door.

It was surprisingly spacious inside, with high ceilings, butcher's block-style tables, and two horseshoe-shaped bars. All the wood was mahogany, and gleamed softly even in the dim light. The smell of fried chicken wings and multiple beers filled the air. The sound of glasses clinking together in celebration reminded her of her late night spell work. She smiled as she walked across the plank flooring past the hostess' station.

Hops and Vines was convenient for both Claire and Teri, almost equidistant between their homes, so it was a meeting place they could easily agree on.

A few businessmen in dark suits, probably somewhere in their fifties, stood close together on the far right side of the bar. Their green and brown beer bottles were clustered on the bar, absorbing the little light in the room as the men laughed together.

A young woman and her likely date sat facing each other on stools a little farther down. Claire sensed an argument as she walked by them. She couldn't hear their muffled conversation, but because she just *knew*.

A few other small groups of people were scattered around the room. She figured the all-male bunch in the corner, wearing tangerine-colored vests and muddied blue jeans, were road workers. Another group consisted of four women in their late forties who'd apparently been dressed by their tween daughters.

Where the hell was Teri? Looking down the length of the bar, Claire finally spotted her, and the group of four men in their late twenties standing directly behind her. Claire's nose immediately picked up the scent: a mixture of Hugo Boss and Drakkar Noir were giving a fair fight to the chicken wings and beer at twenty feet and closing.

Teri was 5'10" to Claire's petite 5'2", and she had long, wavy, caramel-blond hair, slate-blue eyes, and a wide, toothy smile. Claire didn't need a fraction of the gifts she possessed to know that something was coming just by the look on her friend's face. And a moment later, sure as shit, it came.

"Hey!" Teri called out, setting her glass down on the bar with a thunk. "It's the Psychic Network!"

Between the sarcastic remark, and her glassy eyes, it was obvious her friend was already several drinks into her evening.

"Hey, how's the liver holding up?" Claire shot back, not missing a beat. She removed her wool hat and gloves, stuffing them into the pockets of her heavy wool coat before dropping it on the stool next to Teri.

The two women were friends, and had the kind of trust that develops when you're sharing responsibility for massive amounts of machinery and hundreds of human lives, but Claire didn't care for the way that Teri still partied like she was in her twenties, nor did she appreciate the constant cracks. She was, among other things, the daughter of a third-generation medium, which ensured that the gift of spirit communication was well engrained within her genetic makeup. Still, she kept this and her other abilities hidden during her everyday work life. Except, of course, for that one time, and there had been Teri. Teri, who as time passed had revealed herself to be the worst possible person on the planet for Claire to have slipped up in front of.

* * *

Frank, a veteran conductor, was walking through the coaches when he heard the engineer's emergency transmission. He froze in mid-stride.

"Emergency! Emergency! Emergency!" Caleb yelled frantically into the handset. "Emergency! Emergency! Emergency!" he repeated breathlessly, throwing the emergency brakes on.

"Caleb, what happened?" Frank responded over his portable radio, once he was between cars where no passenger could overhear. "Are you all right?"

The train finally ground to a stop with a slow rumbling scrape.

"We hit someone about a half mile back," the engineer replied, trying to catch his breath. Though his body was shaking, he somehow managed to sound calm as he relayed the information to Frank.

Caleb was soaked in sweat, though the cab was a comfortable seventy-three degrees. The moments before the impact replayed incessantly in his mind.

The dispatcher's voice crackled over the engine's radio. "Dispatcher to train number 34, what is the nature of the emergency, over."

"We hit a trespasser at about milepost 116, over."

Frank had followed railroad procedure, and had already secured protection from opposing trains on the adjacent track. He climbed down the trap stairs in the rear of the last coach and began to walk back along the tracks, the way they had come. He carefully maneuvered over the icy ballast as he searched for the body.

About five minutes later, the dispatcher was calling again. "Dispatcher to engineer, train number 34, all rail traffic has been stopped and emergency personnel are en route, over."

"Roger," Caleb replied in a half-whisper, and gently placed the mic back onto its cradle. He had been a locomotive engineer for more than ten years, and had been trained in procedures for pedestrians on the track. Still, nothing had truly prepared him for this.

He sat in the engine's darkened cab for what seemed like forever. Eventually, he saw the flashing red and blue lights of a police car, carefully driving over the ballast alongside the tracks. It was leading a procession of slowly approaching emergency vehicles.

"Conductor train 34 to the engineer, over," Frank huffed. "I can hear the sirens. I'm on my way back; I didn't find anything back here, over."

"Yeah," the engineer replied warily, "There's a whole bunch of people pulling up now." He set the mic back in its cradle as he watched them arrive: three police cars, two ambulances, and three other unmarked cars. They slowly came to a stop, parking in line along the tracks near the engine.

* * *

Eddie Money's "Two Tickets to Paradise" had been replaced on the bar sound system by Edwin Starr's "War."

"WAR! Huh! What is it good for? Absolutely nothing! Say it again…" Claire wondered who the hell was choosing the music.

She felt suddenly anxious, for no reason she could pinpoint. She ran her hand over the back of her bare neck.

Claire's flawless skin never failed to piss Teri off; her friend would constantly complain how unfair it was that her skin looked like that. Which never made any sense to Claire.

"Whaddaya drinking?" Teri asked, slapping her arm.

"Just a club soda," Claire replied.

"Club soda?" Teri's face fell into a disappointed grimace. "I thought we were hanging out?"

"I'm on call," Claire said as she waved over the twenty-something brunette who had been zigzagging back and forth between the two bars. The tension she had begun to feel even before entering the bar was getting worse by the second.

Her arms were itching as though she had walked through a cloud of mosquitos.

"On call?" Teri began sarcastically, as Claire spoke with the chesty waitress. "Is that a road foreman thing, or are those ghosts of yours getting technologically advanced?" she asked with a wide grin. "It's okay," she continued with a shrug, and picked up her drink. "I'm on a mini-vacation starting tomorrow. You can make it up to me."

Claire ignored the flow of jabs until the waitress returned. She smiled at the bubbly girl as she accepted the clear carbonated drink and a small white napkin.

When the waitress walked away, Claire's face became stern. She turned around and focused her full attention on Teri.

"Do you know what a medium is?" she asked, tilting her head to the side and taking a deep breath. Her translucent green eyes locked onto Teri's bloodshot blue ones.

"Hopefully this has something to do with the cheeseburger I ordered," the other woman grumbled.

"Unbelievable," Claire said, looking up at the ceiling for a moment and then forcefully stabbing at the ice in her glass with the small straw.

"Exactly," Teri retorted, rolling her eyes and taking a sip of her drink.

"Why can't you just let that go?" Claire asked, throwing her hands in the air. Clutching her glass, she ignored the man standing behind her stool who kept purposely bumping into her.

"Don't have to," Teri replied with a smirk, setting her drink down on the bar. Claire bit her bottom lip, waiting for the other shoe to drop. Teri was pleased with herself, knowing the hook had been set.

"It's too much fun," she continued. "Whaddaya going to do, turn me into a toad?" She let out a small burp as she finished her sentence, and then looked sheepishly at her friend. There was a palpable silence between them, but then, like many times before over the last three years, they both started laughing.

"Where'd the waitress go?" Teri asked, looking away toward the other end of the bar.

Claire stared at her friend and rubbed her bottom lip thoughtfully. "I'll turn you into a toad, all right," she quipped, just below the threshold of audibility.

* * *

Caleb opened the fireman's, or passenger's-side, door and stuck his head out into the frigid late-afternoon air. Shivering, he grabbed the handles on the locomotive's ladder and made his way down to the ground.

The busy emergency personnel were unaware of his presence. When he reached the front of the engine, he caught a glimpse of something strange in his peripheral vision and glanced at the face of the locomotive. His eyes widened and tears formed. He felt his throat closing, and his breath stopped in his lungs.

The body was impaled on the train's knuckle—the coupler that allowed the locomotive to connect to another train car. He could see one of the lifeless hands, suspended in midair and dangling down toward the tracks. They were the most eerie shade of blue he had ever seen.

Everything seemed to be happening in slow motion. "That's the engineer! Don't let him see this! Get him out of here!" someone cried.

Caleb felt bile fill his throat in a wave, and bent over to release it all in a hot gush, splattering between his boots. He stood and wiped his mouth on his sleeve and slowly walked back to the side of the engine. He crawled up the ladder, and pulled himself back inside. After shutting the engine door and returning to his seat, he reached up and turned off the lights in the cab. He lowered his head into his trembling hands, his body going limp as though trapped under thousands of pounds of sand. Tears began flowing down his reddened cheeks. *I killed someone.*

* * *

Claire's work ringtone began to chime, and she grabbed her phone off the bar.

"I gotta take this," she said, pressing the talk button and covering her other ear to block the music. "This is Claire," she said, and listened to the frenzied words coming from the other end. "Okay. Okay. I'll be there."

When she had interviewed for the road foreman's position, many of the answers had come easily to her based on her experience as an engineer. She had studied things like reading an engine's download tapes, measuring wheels, using a radar gun, monitoring fuel consumption, and train handling prior to coming, and had breezed through the tests. She had come to understand that the hardest aspect of the job was dealing with the unexpected—like being on call for emergency situations such as this one.

Seeing her friend's expression change, Teri stopped smiling and quietly began swirling the ice cubes in her glass with the straw. She pushed them down into the liquid one at a time. She sat quietly for a moment, and looked casually around the room. The man standing behind her had an incredibly perfect ass. She grinned and swung back around on her stool, facing the bar. Taking another sip of her drink, she waited for Claire to wrap up her call.

Sticking her phone in her pocket, Claire grabbed her coat from the back of the stool and slipped into it.

"Everything all right?" Teri asked, with genuine concern. Claire was staying calm, but there was something dark in her eyes.

"No," she answered, grabbing her wool hat and pulling it down over her coal-black hair. Ignoring the attractive man behind her who was still trying to get her attention, she sighed.

"Someone die?" Teri asked uneasily. She knew how hard fatality investigations were on her friend, but never believed any of the stories Claire would tell her about them afterward.

Teri didn't believe in certain things, and high on that list was the idea of dead people talking. If you broached the subject, she would never, ever let it go. Claire had learned that the hard way. But she would still tell her friend "Casper Stories," as Teri dismissively referred to them, regardless.

"Yes," Claire answered quickly.

"Where?"

"Muir's Mountain," Claire replied. "I'm sorry, but I have—"

Teri cut her off. "Get out of here." She smacked Claire on the arm. "And I don't want to hear any paranormal activity shit when you get back."

Claire rubbed her hands together, staring down at Teri's glass. Then she smiled and glanced back up at her friend. "I'll deal with you later, toad," she said with a wink.

Disappointed by the early end to their girls' night, but completely understanding about the reason behind it, Teri flagged down the waitress. She picked up her glass to take a final sip, and immediately noticed three black flies squirming around inside it.

"What the hell?" she said, disgusted, and dropped it to the bar, where it fell over and slowly rolled sideways, a trickle of alcohol and melting ice leaking onto the dark wood.

CHAPTER 3

THE APPARITION

When Claire arrived on the scene, pulses of red and blue light from the emergency vehicles illuminated her car's path through the woods toward the train. The thermostat on her car told her it was twelve below zero outside. Claire glanced at it unhappily as she spoke to another manager on her cell.

"Yes," Dave, the crew management officer, replied. "Relief crew is en route, I believe."

"Okay, thank you," Claire said and ended the call. She turned off the car, put her wool hat and gloves back on and donned a company-issued hardhat. She slid her laptop into her backpack and extracted a pair of safety glasses from the glove compartment. Radio in hand, she hopped out of the car into the frigid evening.

She kept her "to-go bag" in the trunk. Opening the plastic bag, she removed a pair of heavy-duty engineer's boots that she only wore when investigating trespasser incidents. She slipped them on, placing her dress boots on the floor in the car's back seat. She tossed her winter coat in after them, after putting on a federally mandated green florescent parka.

It was important to always have a separate set of clothing when investigating railroad fatalities. Claire knew she would more than likely find herself walking over what is known as a debris field. Bodily fluids and parts would cover a long stretch of track, having flown in all directions following impact with the train. She obviously didn't want to be tracking that through her house—beyond being disgusting, it was a biological hazard. Zipping up her shiny green jacket, she headed down the icy path to investigate the trespasser incident.

A heavyset man in a bulky black parka with florescent yellow stripes noticed her and quickly started walking in her direction.

"Ma'am," the officer said, holding his badge up for her to see. "This is an emergency situation; you're going to have to leave."

Claire nodded at him. "Yes, officer, I know. My name is Claire Montgomery and I'm the road foreman responsible for this crew," she said, raising her own company badge for *him* to inspect.

"Oh, okay," he said, lifting it to take a closer look and offering no apology for assuming she was just some gawker.

"Do you have any questions for me, officer?"

"No, actually, we should be wrapping things up pretty soon," he replied, handing her badge back to her as he took a tissue from his pocket and rubbed his nose.

"Did you already speak with my engineer?" she asked.

"Yes. We have everything we need in that respect. Sounds like a suicide," he concluded somberly. He glanced at the engine for a moment, and leaned in closer. "The conductor was throwing up pretty bad; the whole scene messed him up pretty good."

"Where is he?" she asked, following his gaze toward the train.

The officer shrugged. "Probably still got his head in the bushes," he replied, raising his eyebrows.

Claire nodded and held her hand out to the officer. "Thank you very much, officer, I'm going to head up to see the engineer." He shook her hand and walked back to the front of the engine where most of the emergency personnel were gathered.

Standing on the snow- and ice-covered ballast at the bottom of the ladder on the side of the engine, Claire spoke into her portable radio.

"Mobile unit 321 calling engineer, train number 34. I'm at the bottom of the ladder, I'm coming up, over." The frigid wind whipped her face as she looked up the side of the engine. Interviewing traumatized engineers was always the hardest part of her investigations.

The door leading into the cab remained closed. Claire stuck the radio in her coat pocket and swung the backpack over her shoulder. She grabbed the handles on either side of the ladder and climbed up the six steps.

"Hey, there," she said as she stepped through the door into the cab. The engineer barely raised his head in acknowledgment.

Claire removed her hardhat and safety glasses and took a seat on the fireman's chair, about two feet across from him. The cab was freezing cold and dark inside. The engineer was probably suffering from shock and anxiety, as well as a rise in blood pressure, and didn't seem affected.

The authorities were in the grim process of removing the corpse from the knuckle, which required that the power be turned off. Even in sub-zero temperatures, it was necessary in a situation like this.

"Have you been drinking water? It helps with the adrenaline," Claire offered. Her words left her mouth wrapped in clouds of frozen breath.

The engineer sat silent, staring down at the console. Claire knew he had been crying and was trying to pull himself together. Respecting his process, she turned her attention to the control panel on the cab's back wall.

The control panel is the railroad equivalent of an airplane's black box. She began downloading the engine data onto her laptop. The engineer remained quiet and still as she worked.

As Claire was wrapping up the download and analysis, Caleb began to dry heave. He spewed a green, watery liquid all over the floor and console.

She put down the laptop and scurried through a narrow door behind his seat. Snatching some paper towels from the engine's bathroom, she rushed back into the cab to mop up as best she could.

There was a bottle of water in the engine's refrigerator. She grabbed it and handed it to him, placing a gentle hand on his shoulder as he tried to take a sip.

"I've checked out the download," she said. "There's nothing you could have done differently. You did it by the book, Caleb; it's not your fault."

His bloodshot eyes briefly shifted her way. She could see the heartbreak in his gaze.

"Why don't you go back and have a seat in the coaches," she suggested. "You don't need to watch any of this stuff."

Caleb nodded and stood up from the engineer's seat. Opening the fireman's-side door, he carefully grabbed the sides of the ladder and descended to the ground.

Claire looked out the open door and watched as he made his way over the icy ballast back toward the coaches. She hoped that Frank, the conductor, had straightened up and announced the problem to the passengers in a way that would keep everyone patient and compliant. While most people understand that trains don't go looking for people to hit, when it happens it's traumatic for everyone involved.

As she shut the door to the engine, the hair on the back of her neck started to rise. She turned around and looked across the cab. Where the engineer had been moments ago, a figure in silhouette now stood.

It was a young girl, in maybe her mid-teens. The presence flickered like a hologram. She was there, yet not.

Something outside caught Claire's eye. She looked through the large windshield.

About fifty feet in front of the engine, the girl who had been impaled by the knuckle lay on a gurney. Her oozing guts had left a disturbing trail of flesh in the snow. Yet that same girl was also now standing inside the engine, staring blankly at her. Suddenly, Claire heard a voice in her mind. It was not her voice, nor was it a thought she'd have had on her own.

"*I have been waiting,*" the girl told Claire. Her words were muffled at first.

Claire stared at her. She focused her mind and answered the girl aloud.

"Waiting for what?" she asked.

The silhouette remained silent.

"You were in the middle of the tracks," Claire said. "The horn was blowing and you just stood there. I am sorry, but you are dead."

This wasn't the first time a spirit had lingered on this side and needed Claire to tell them that he or she had died. There was another long moment of silence as they stared across the cab at each other. Claire was acutely aware of her breaths becoming puffs of steam as they left her mouth. Mostly because that wasn't happening with the presence on the other side of the cab.

Claire was now beginning to receive thoughts from the girl. They sounded distant at first, like a poorly tuned radio signal that you have to adjust for a while.

Spirit communication operates that way, like a two-way radio. But, just like a radio, sometimes a crappy channel is just a crappy channel. What *was* coming through was confusing. Claire could hear the young girl saying that she was finally free and no longer scared. This was nothing like other conversations she'd had with suicides. The odd-ness of it was giving her a strange sensation deep in her gut.

The information was bombarding her now. She began to feel lightheaded, overwhelmed by the sheer volume of it. It was a flood of images, feelings, and emotions, raw and unfiltered, pour-ing out like water from a burst pipe.

Why were you on the tracks, in the middle of the woods, on such a cold day?, Claire interjected mentally.

The girl's reply was too fast to catch; some of the words were in broken English, and others were in a language Claire didn't know. Russian, maybe?

"Slow down," Claire murmured. *I am having a hard time keeping up with you.*

Christine was the name the spirit called herself. She thought she was 13 but wasn't sure. She had been abused in a mountainside house since she was 9, maybe 8. She was *frozen*; she wasn't on the tracks. She *thawed. Little John, he's in danger, little John, little John. Little John. I was waiting. Oh no, he is coming. He's on the train.*

Who is coming? Is someone here to meet you?, Claire asked, but the connection was suddenly broken. The information that had slowly been assembling on the screen in her mind's eye began to scramble.

A cold breeze quickly wafted past her. Claire knew it was the portal, and that meant Christine was about to cross over. The volume of her voice began to drop, like when you turn down the knob on a radio. Her ghostly silhouette began to fade and become translucent. It was as though Christine was being vacuumed up into nothingness.

An abrupt knocking rattled the fireman's-side door. Caught by surprise, Claire bit her bottom lip. She shook her head violently as though she had just taken too big a bite of ice cream. The door opened, and a burst of frigid air entered the cab, followed by Frank's pale face.

"Hey," he said, his voice shaking. "Is the relief crew here? I need to get out of here. I just need to get out of here."

"They'll be here soon," Claire replied sympathetically. Frank retreated back outside and slammed the door.

It was strange, she thought, that Frank looked more shaken as things were starting to wrap up than he had when she'd first arrived. Thank goodness he and the assistant conductor were being relieved soon.

She reached into her backpack for a small spiral notebook. Detaching a pen from her ID lanyard, she began to scribble notes as fast as she could. She was trying to remember everything Christine had told her—and there was a lot to remember.

Though she was relieved that the girl hadn't needed help to cross over, the exchange troubled her. Claire had been communicating with spirits for more than twenty years, and had always been able to get a complete sense of what they were trying to convey. Usually she found that people's stories were very well rounded at the end of their lives. This encounter had felt all wrong. *What the hell was she waiting for?* Who *was here?*

Frank's quivering voice came over the radio and she looked up.

"Conductor train 34 to Road Foreman Montgomery. You can turn the head end power back on, everyone is in the clear."

"Roger. Here it comes," Claire replied. She pushed in the large blue knob on the engine's control panel to restore the electricity. A moment later, the lights and heat restarted with a loud and comforting hum.

The police released the train just as the relief crew was pulling up to the incident scene. Claire gathered her laptop and notebook and returned them to the backpack.

"*Little John,*" she whispered to herself. She wondered how she could find out more about the girl, but knew there would be no further communication. Once someone had successfully crossed over, the communication ended in that moment and with that act. Usually, it is the spirit who comes to the medium when it needs to talk with a loved one still in this realm. But for a medium to contact a spirit, a loved one must be present. Claire didn't know why it worked that way, but in her experience, it had always been like that, with no exceptions.

She climbed out of the engine and down to the ground. Darkness had fallen.

The emergency vehicles' flashing lights had been replaced by a succession of red taillights slowly leaving the scene and following one another out of the woods. It was almost like an eerie, pre-funeral procession, railroad style.

This type of procession had been occurring since the inception of the railroad itself. For a seemingly endless variety of reasons, almost all of them macabre, people were forever drawn to the tracks.

Claire returned to her own vehicle, shivering. She knew something was wrong and needed to talk to someone about it, but whom could she tell? If she tried to explain it to the police, their first question would be, "Are you currently taking any medications?"

Teri? That would be like asking a vegan for advice on how to season a holiday rib roast. But there was no choice. Teri was a loud and annoying skeptic, but she was a friend, and Claire trusted her implicitly.

She got in the car, turned the engine over and cranked the heat. Taking her cell phone out, she called Teri. She shook her head, grinning at her friend's first words.

"Lemme guess—you *knew* I was thinking about you, right?"

CHAPTER 4

QUEST FOR ANSWERS

"I need you to be serious. This fatality wasn't like the rest," Claire said as she entered Teri's apartment.

Teri took one look at her friend's face and lost her sarcastic grin.

"What is it? What happened?"

Claire stood, staring at her. "I don't know; I really don't know," she said. "It was a young teenage girl, and she didn't know what had happened to her. I told her that she'd been hit by a train. But she told me that she was *frozen, thawed,* and *wasn't there.* There was something about a little boy named John, and a guy named Doug not being the only one." Claire rubbed her forehead. The more she thought about it, the more exhausted she felt. "I don't understand. I really don't."

"Understand what?" Teri asked.

"I have never had this happen," Claire answered. "I wish my grandmother or my mom were still alive to help. They would probably know what was going on. But they aren't..." Her voice trailed off as she glanced over at Teri.

"You aren't making any sense," Teri said. "I mean, even by your usual Ghost Whisperer standards, you're not making any sense."

"I just don't know," Claire said. "I felt her relief. She didn't care that she was gone. But she kept talking about this *Little John*. She was just crossing over when the conductor, who was a complete spazz case, came into the cab of the engine and shocked me out of the conversation, so that was all I got." Claire knew she wasn't really making herself clear, and she felt like she was moving and speaking in slow motion. "This is really different."

"The dead person said what now? Start again from the beginning," Teri said as she walked into the kitchen and turned on the coffee maker. Although she had been enjoying the buzz she had maintained since Claire had left her behind at Hops and Vines, she knew she needed to get it together. Moving a few things around in the cluttered kitchen sink, Teri managed to find two mugs and washed them out as she waited for the coffee to brew.

"Do you want tea or coffee?" she called, as she rummaged noisily through the kitchen.

"You know I can't drink that stuff at night. Do you have any soda? If not, water is fine," Claire replied. She restacked a precarious, three-foot pile of laundry on the light-green sofa, making a place for herself to sit.

She waited for a smart-ass remark as Teri walked back into the living room and handed her a mug of water, but it never came. Maybe it was the look on Claire's face that was holding her friend's attitude in check, but Teri kept her mouth shut. Sitting on the mismatched blue loveseat across from Claire, wearing pink sweats and a gray hoodie, she took a sip of coffee and stared at her friend in silence. Claire looked back at her for a moment and then continued.

"Okay," she said. "Once the engineer left, that's when the spirit of the girl who was hit started communicating. She was talking fast. I took down five pages of notes and I still don't think I got it all. She had an accent, maybe Russian, I don't know. She told me that she had been held captive for a long time, and there was another kid involved. It sounded like a crime, like they were kidnapped or something. But I don't need anyone thinking that I've lost my marbles," she sighed. "I just don't need that shit."

Teri realized that every last vestige of her buzz had dissipated, and she didn't think it had anything to do with the two swallows of coffee she'd had. She found her friend's story genuinely unnerving. Not because someone had died. People died on the tracks all the time. It was because she couldn't push away the uneasy feeling that this Casper Story might be true.

Teri had taken jabs at Claire since the Cayenne Pepper Incident. She thought the stories her friend told her, and the assertions she made about being able to do magic—with or without a "k" at the end—were bullshit, figments of Claire's imagination. Or, failing that, things that could be explained by logic or science. It was like figuring out how someone made a card disappear; chances are, they'd just distracted you by waving their other hand.

"There's one more thing," Claire said hesitantly, knowing she would probably live to regret it.

"What's that?" Teri asked, taking another sip of coffee.

"She gave me an address."

CHAPTER 5

ANYBODY HOME?

The St. Albans Library was very busy for a Friday morning. A bunch of teens were gathered near the main entrance, where the few available computers stood; the library had Internet access, but no wi-fi. The nearby chairs and tables were covered with their textbooks and laptops. The way the kids were hopping around from one terminal to another, in animated conversation, it looked like a social event.

The library's local section was tucked away in a small alcove. It contained a lot of history, including books by local authors and artifacts in glass cases, as well as several decades' worth of newspapers on microfiche. Claire headed straight for the area, hoping to find something that would help her make sense of Christine's words.

She began her research with the address Christine had given her: 421 Milton Springs Road. She amassed all the information she could find in a pile on the table, but instead of poring over the papers, she sat silently staring at the pile. Hoping that something would provoke an emotional ping, or better yet, a mental image, she waited.

Claire's ability to receive such signs had developed when she was very young. She remembered her mom asking her, "Claire, what happens when you turn a light on in the dark?"

Sitting in their small, inadequately heated apartment in her tiny jeans and sweater, she had answered, "The darkness disappears."

Her mom had smiled and gently patted her head.

Claire had loved playing games with her mother, and learning to hone her special skills. Mom had trained her with a deck of playing cards that bore pictures of women holding trays of Coca-Cola.

"Okay, Claire, is this red or black?" her mother would ask, flopping a card face-down on the table in front of her.

The card-guessing game took place a few days a week until, after several months, Claire realized that by touching the card, she could *feel* whether it was red or black. As her abilities grew, the tests grew more difficult: her mom would ask how many symbols were on the card, or if it had a picture of a person on it.

The game was fun, but Claire knew it wasn't something that the other kids played. Her mother told her never to talk about it with her friends, and she didn't.

When she was about 9, her mother taught her the People Game.

This game was played with information that Claire got as little pictures in her head, or sometimes as a particularly pressing thought.

"Tell me who you think is visiting us today, Claire?" her mother would ask, nudging her gently.

"It's Uncle Bill," Claire would happily state. Then her mother would ask her to describe him, and then ask which side of the family he belonged to.

She learned to arrange the mental pictures in her mind, to push them around like she was moving pieces on a chessboard. The left side was for her father's family, and the right side was for her mother's. Claire also pictured them on stairs, so she could tell which generation they belonged to. If they were of the same generation as her mom, they would be on the second step; her nana's generation would be on the third step, and so on.

"Remember, Claire, you need to tell me at least five things about this person. I need to know beyond a shadow of doubt who is visiting," her mom would always say.

I hope I can remember everything, she remembered whispering to herself as she looked up toward the ceiling, wanting badly to please her mother.

Claire sighed as she came back to the present. She stared at the pile of documents for hours, ignoring glances from other library patrons. Nothing was happening. She wasn't getting any visual images, or any pings on her senses. Most of the material she'd gathered was area maps— until she happened to glance at a real-estate transfer that had occurred in June 2011 in the town of Milton. *The tracks run through Milton*, she thought. She jotted down the name of the owner of 421 Milton Springs Road.

After discovering that tidbit, though, she slammed into a dead end. Everything from August 30, 2011 forward seemed to be nonstop coverage of Hurricane Irene. Claire began putting away the stacks of material she had accumulated.

She left the library and headed for a nearby park, looking for a quiet bench. Most of them were covered in ice and snow. The only bench she could find was small and rickety, and tucked behind a frozen fountain. It was partially cleared, though, and she had cell service.

She pulled up a photo of 421 Milton Springs Road on her phone and looked at it. It was an old photo, and a nondescript house. But she knew differently.

That's where Little John is, Claire whispered to herself. *Is he who she was waiting for?* She took out her notebook and began to go over everything she had written down after communicating with

Christine. *What in the hell does "thawed" mean? Warmed up by the fire?*

Though the information that had flowed from Christine to Claire was telepathic in nature, it came across no differently than a telephone conversation that sometimes has connection problems. Claire sighed, and began to review her notes.

Christine and Little John had been kept in a big house on a hill. They had been confined to the house and forbidden, or prevented, from leaving the property. Doug, and someone he called Delivery Boy, had treated them brutally. *We didn't eat for days when we first got here. We were kept in a room without windows and no toilet. He was starving us. John was little and so hungry I wasn't sure he would be able to make it much longer without food. Doug would lock the doors and only let us out to clean and make him dinner.*

Christine's legs and back were often black and blue. She had pulled Doug off of Little John once, as he was breaking the boy's legs, and after that she suffered frequent and vicious beatings herself. Her own right arm and left foot had never fully healed from the attacks.

Claire winced as she finished reading. Closing the notebook and taking out her phone, she opened up Google Earth and got directions to the address. Oddly, they stopped at an area, not a street. When she zoomed in to Street View, no houses were visible in the surrounding area.

"That's not possible," she said, furrowing her brow. She stood up from the bench and walked across the park, crunching over the ice and snow toward her car. "Something's missing."

CHAPTER 6

FOR THE RECORD

Claire could feel a picture forming in her mind's eye, but it didn't make sense. It came again as she got into her car: dust, dirt, or something like it. No, it wasn't dirt; it was pulsing and shifting, more like the gray static you would see on a television forty years ago, after the station had gone off the air for the night. "The bug fights," they used to call it.

A few people were walking through the park, all bundled up. She ignored them, started the car and drove south out of town. As she passed a dilapidated drive-in theater on her left, she thought about Teri.

Her friend had managed to act supportive, and Claire had been thankful for that, but she held out little hope that Teri would ever believe in a reality beyond the one she knew.

It was understandable. As a child, Teri's parents had dragged her into what she would only ever refer to as a "fad religious cult." She'd never told Claire about it in detail, and Claire had never pushed the issue. Whatever had happened, as an adult, Teri was not only estranged from her father (her mother was dead) but shunned anyone that even smelled like organized religion. On her worst days, she was about one step away from spitting at nuns in the street.

Claire thought it ironic that they'd met while she was in the middle of a ritual. That they had become the closest of friends despite that surprised both of them. Still, whenever Claire would talk about anything that had a spiritual element, she knew that Teri was simply enduring it for friendship's sake and nothing more. The fact that Teri would get a look like Claire had forced her to take a bite of a sandwich made with warm lard, old cigarette butts, and parmesan cheese was a big hint. It didn't matter how many times Claire tried to explain that there was nothing negative about witchcraft. Teri didn't want to hear about it; she just waited for Claire to let it drop.

It was a beautiful ride up to Milton. The ice-covered rocks, scattered between the tall, snow-capped trees, had a bluish tint that lit up the scenery like holiday decorations. It reminded Claire of the first time she had seen the enormous Christmas tree in Rockefeller Center, some thirty years ago. It was mesmerizing. But as she wound further up the mountainside, the clouds began to darken and her feeling of awe was slowly replaced with a sense of isolation.

She was coming around a curve, a hard rocky slope on one side and a sharp fall down the mountain on the other, when her tires began to slip. She'd hit a patch of black ice in the road. Claire calmly took her foot off the gas pedal and waited for the car to correct itself. *One perk of living in a place where winter can quickly bring extreme conditions is that you are prepared for most situations,* she thought.

Most situations, she repeated to herself as she stopped the car and looked out the window. She was at the top of the mountain, where 421 Milton Springs Road was supposed to be on every app and piece of paper she could unearth. But it wasn't there.

Claire stepped out of the car, inhaling the crisp, cold air. No one was coming up the road behind her, and she stood staring straight ahead. She could easily see a mile in every direction.

This is a mistake. It has to be, she said to herself, bewildered as she turned in a slow circle, taking in everything around her. Young pine trees learning to stand under the weight of the snow, and large rocks covered in ice: That was it, for as far as the eye could see.

In Claire's experience, spirits didn't make mistakes. Their communications were always deliberate and specific. Everything meant something. Did they sometimes give hints instead of direct answers? Sure. Did they sometimes use symbolism instead of words? Yes, of course. But what they didn't do, what they *never* did, was get something as concrete as an address wrong.

"Absurd," Claire mumbled, climbing back into the car. She rubbed her hands together, blowing her warm breath between her palms. After a few minutes, she carefully turned the car around and began to head back down the mountain, cautious of the ice she now knew was hiding on the road.

A sense of urgency was beginning to well within her. *Little John. I have to find him.* As she traveled down the mountainside, Claire was no longer paying attention to the scenery. She was focused on the question of why Christine's spirit had been so certain of the address—421 Milton Springs Road. Milton Springs ran up the mountain, and 421 would have been pretty much dead center at the top of it. Claire knew she'd been in the right spot. But it was nothing but empty space.

The tracks are at the base of the mountain, and that's where Christine was. She said 421 Milton Springs Road…she said it.

Claire knew something was wrong.

Reaching the bottom of the mountain, she made a left and headed back toward town.

It was three in the afternoon. *City Hall will still be open,* she thought. But her stomach was grumbling as she approached a small strip mall that included a drugstore, an ice cream parlor, a burger place, and a coffee shop.

She made a right into the parking lot and pulled up in front of the old-fashioned burger shack's window. *She said that was where she lived. What am I missing?*

Stepping out of the car with the motor still running, Claire ordered a cheeseburger with a side of steak fries and then jumped back in the car. There were picnic tables scattered about, and during the summer they'd be full of families eating lunch. But this was the dead of winter. It was left entirely up to you to order and wait in your car, or if you were stupid, wait outside and freeze to death. She peeled out of the parking lot as soon as the chubby teenage cashier handed her the steaming bag of food.

Setting the bag on the passenger seat, she fished around inside it with her right hand as she drove, grabbing hot, oily fries and stuffing them into her mouth. She didn't like eating in her car, but wasn't about to miss her chance to enter City Hall just because she'd wanted a cheeseburger.

She pulled up in front of the old brick building, grateful to find a parking space only a short walk from its wide cement steps. Climbing out of the car, she pumped three quarters into the meter with one hand and popped one last fry into her mouth with the other. She crossed the sidewalk and trotted up the steps and through the imposing white wooden doors into the building.

Government buildings always had the same nondescript smell, no matter where you found yourself. It wasn't a good or a bad smell; it was just sort of…there, and slightly odd. Claire always noticed smells, and ever since that night, over thirty years ago, she couldn't let go of one without labeling it in her mind. It was an affliction of sorts.

She spotted a large, glass-encased bulletin board hanging on the wall to her left, listing the various offices and their corresponding room numbers. The Office of Public Records was 201. She walked across the white marble floor to the elevator, pressed the button and waited. Just as she stepped into the car, she heard the *Jaws* theme: the ringtone she had selected for Teri. She pulled the cell from her pocket and answered it.

"Hey," she said, taking a breath and trying to hide her anxiety. She didn't really want to talk to Teri, of all people, until she had some real answers.

"Hi," Teri said. "How are you making—"

The line suddenly went dead. The elevator doors opened onto the second floor, where Claire turned her phone off and dropped it back into her pocket as she stepped out into the quiet hallway. Straight across from her was room 201. As she entered, a woman wearing black-rimmed glasses, easily in her seventies, came to the counter.

"What can I help you with, dear?"

"Hopefully solving a bit of a mystery," Claire replied with her friendliest smile. "I'm looking for a house that was supposed to be at this address." She offered the piece of paper with *421 Milton Springs Road* written across the top.

The woman scribbled down the address with a nod, and walked away.

Claire sat on a frayed blue chair across from the door and waited. As she sat, she began to try to identify that distinctive government-building smell. It was bothering her. *Stucco and olive oil? Maybe wet paint and a touch of pine oil?* She was really on a roll by the time the woman returned.

"Well, dear," the woman began as she opened a large manila folder. "Four-twenty-one Milton Springs Road used to be the address of an old Victorian home. Unfortunately, on August 30, 2011 Hurricane Irene destroyed quite a few properties in this area. Four twenty-one was one of them."

"What?" Claire leaned over the counter as the older woman pointed to the information on the sheet.

"That's been gone for years, dear, see?"

Claire slowly stood upright as the woman closed the folder.

"Have a nice day, dear," she said as she walked away.

Claire was speechless. She sat back down in the blue chair, shaking her head and slowly rubbing her palms together.

The older woman returned with a concerned look on her face. "Sweetheart, are you all right? You look like you've seen a ghost."

"Or *didn't*," Claire murmured uneasily.

"You didn't what, dear?"

"Nothing, sorry." Claire headed for the door, gently closing it behind her.

She wasn't really there? Claire could feel her head beginning to pound. After all, what proof did she have of anything Christine had said, beyond that of her own senses?

Am I losing my mind? She felt real fear for the first time in decades. Stopping at the elevator door, she pressed the down button and closed her eyes tightly.

Talk to me, she demanded in her mind.

Nothing.

Talk to me, damn it, she thought again.

Nothing.

The elevator door opened and she stepped inside. Pressing 1, she leaned back against the wall as the door closed.

Her mind began to race. *It couldn't have happened*, she thought. *She couldn't have really been on that engine if the house didn't exist that day. So, what—I hallucinated? I'm having hallucinations now?*

She began to think about more than twenty years of spirit communications, bombarding her mind with all her past experiences, looking for one piece of hard evidence that her perceptions had been real.

Nothing. Nothing anyone could physically touch, anyway. She could feel herself beginning to panic. The elevator door opened and she leapt out. Walking as fast as she could she crossed the sidewalk and climbed back into her car.

The thought of Teri's response hit her like a boulder landing on her chest.

"I've been trying to tell you this for years," her friend was sure to say, her scorn almost certain to be followed by, "I knew all that crap was bullshit. So what kinda meds they got ya on?"

Claire began to feel nauseated. Were her abilities betraying her? Had they ever existed at all? What did her life even mean, if it had all been a lie?

Suddenly, her grandmother's voice floated into her mind. *"Do not question yourself. The present is liquid."*

Holy shit, that isn't even my voice. I'm schizophrenic? She sat paralyzed with fear, hands wrapped tightly around the steering wheel.

"Breathe, Claire, just breathe," she murmured. After a few minutes, her breathing had calmed and the panic had dissipated. But her confidence and trust were now replaced by one of the darkest forces she had ever encountered...doubt.

CHAPTER 7

SECOND GUESSING

Claire walked into her condo. It was very cozy, the perfect counterpoint to the metal and grime that surrounded her at work. It was small and clean, and scented with an herbal potpourri she had mixed herself: a blend of rosemary, sage, lemon balm, pine, and lavender laurel. A whiff greeted her as she walked down the entry hall and into the living room. She slipped off her winter boots and parked them behind the dark-brown reclining sofa. Once again, the *Jaws* theme swelled through her phone's speaker.

She didn't answer. Taking the phone out of her coat pocket and placing it atop the coffee table, she walked across the room to the electric fireplace. She scrolled through the choices on the remote's atmosphere selector, opting for a subdued blue flame. She lit the two white taper candles perched on corners of the mantle and headed for the couch.

The house was quiet. Coal, her long-haired black cat, padded over to greet her, rubbing her side and little gray tush against Claire's calf. Claire picked up her fifty-inch flat screen TV's remote and put her feet up on the coffee table.

She rolled her eyes as the *Jaws* theme started again. Her patience exhausted, she grabbed the phone.

"What?" Claire snapped. "How could you tell that you were right? Are *you* psychic?"

Teri recoiled, staring at the phone in confusion for a moment before putting it back up to her ear. She stretched out on her couch, laying her feet beside a pile of unfolded clothes.

"What seems to be the problem?" Teri asked, acting barely affected by Claire's dig. "Did I interrupt you while *Long Island Medium* was on?" She laughed.

"You're really something, Teri," Claire said in an even tone. "You win, I'm a fake. Goodbye."

Twenty minutes later, the knock at Claire's front door was neither welcome nor a surprise. She tipped her head back against the couch, staring at the ceiling in aggravation as Teri continued knocking, first on the door and then on the window.

Teri's muffled voice could be heard through the pounding. "You know I'm not leaving. I'm not going to break my knuckles on this door, either. I'm about thirty seconds away from finding a nice dirty rock to use instead. Your choice."

Claire threw her hands up with a sigh of exasperation and rose from the couch. She walked across the Berber carpet to the front door and unlocked it without opening it.

Teri came in pissed off. "What the hell was that all about?" she asked coldly.

Claire had already drunk a few glasses of wine, and as far as she was concerned, she was nowhere near done. She raised her glass to her lips, and then stopped.

"I may need professional help," she muttered before taking a long drink.

"For what?" Teri asked. "You just finished the carpeting—did a pipe burst or something?" She furrowed her brow and stretched her neck to stare into Claire's kitchen.

"No," Claire said softly, taking another swallow of wine. Her hands were beginning to tremble. She set the glass back down on the coffee table.

Teri knew that her friend rarely drank, and she absolutely *never* drank alone. This had something to do with the psychic stuff, but she didn't know what.

"It wasn't there," Claire said, shrugging and staring at the carpet, not making eye contact. "Hasn't even existed since 2011."

"What wasn't there?" Teri asked.

"Four-twenty-one Milton Springs Road. The address the spirit gave me. It was part of the destruction from Irene, one of many homes destroyed. So go ahead, take your best shot."

A single tear slid slowly down Claire's cheek. She wiped it away with the back of her hand, and cleared her throat.

"Why the hell are you crying? Because a house wasn't where it was supposed to be?" Teri scolded. "That's ridiculous, Claire. You in your cycle or something?" In her own way, she was trying to cheer her friend up. But even she could sense that there were larger ramifications.

"No, it's more than that. Because that house not being there means that I'm hallucinating—that maybe none of what I've believed all these years has been real," Claire blurted.

"Okay, so lemme get this straight. You think that you're ill because some spirit got its information mixed up?" Teri unzipped her brown, wool-collared bomber jacket and sat on the couch next to her friend.

"You don't understand, Teri," Claire said, shaking her head in frustration and looking sullenly down at the floor. "Spirits don't get these things *wrong*."

"There's a first time for everything, babe," Teri said with a soft chuckle, and laid a hand on Claire's shoulder.

Claire glared at her friend. "Why are you being supportive about something you don't believe in yourself?"

Teri shrugged and stood up. "I don't have to believe it. You do, and you're my friend. That's enough. And when you have something you really believe in, you don't just walk away from it, Claire." The two women stared at each other for a moment, then Teri shrugged and walked back toward the door, zipping her jacket against the cold. As she was leaving, she called over her shoulder, "If you still have me on your phone as *Jaws*, I'm gonna kick your ass."

Claire giggled as Teri closed the door behind her. A moment later, she heard the *Jaws* theme coming from her phone.

"I friggin' knew it!" Teri yelled through the door, but there was laughter in her voice, too.

CHAPTER 8

Restoring Communications

Coal's loud, rhythmic purring and warm puffs of breath on her face woke Claire. She had fallen asleep on the couch after finishing off a bottle of Merlot, and the cat was curled snugly around her neck.

Claire gently pulled Coal off, set her on the cushion, and sat up. She looked over at the clock on the TV screen; it was after seven. Morning already.

Christine and Little John popped into her mind as she walked through the small dining room into the kitchen.

Teri was right, she said to herself, scooping the blueberry coffee grounds into the filter bed. *There's something off, and it might not be me.*

Three days had passed since the accident, but it didn't feel that way to her. It felt like one really long, shitty day.

Well, today is a new day, she told herself and tried out a smile. She started the coffee maker and turned the radio on. Christopher Cross' "Sailing" was playing. Though it was nowhere near her taste, she left it alone. Claire was a fan of heavier stuff, Metallica and the like, but today was different. Many things were different.

She opened the front door to grab the day's newspaper from the porch, but it was just out of reach. She often thought the little jerk paperboy did it on purpose. But by stretching her bare foot across the snow, she was able to grab it with her toes and pull it to her.

As she stepped back inside the condo, she froze. An abrupt and premonitory feeling began to seize her. Her hands trembled and she clutched the newspaper tighter.

The mellow strains of "Sailing" had stopped midstream, and the radio had switched to a different song. One phrase started to play over and over again. "Ice, ice, baby. Ice, ice, baby." Claire slowly walked back to the kitchen, not knowing what she would see or encounter, but when she reentered the room, "Sailing" resumed.

She looked down at the newspaper in her hands. Taking it out of its orange plastic bag, she unfolded it on the farmhouse-style kitchen table. She poured herself a cup of coffee and leaned against the countertop, looking quizzically at it.

Spirits sometimes choose indirect methods of communication. If a person is practiced and open, it is easy to pick up on. But you first had to set aside any notion of coincidence. In Claire's experience, it didn't exist. She sat down and scanned the front page. Something about the president's latest executive order, and a few other national stories, but nothing that popped out at her.

I am nuts, she thought, closing the paper and then tossing it away from her, onto the counter.

A few minutes later, she heard the *Jaws* theme and returned to the living room to get her phone.

"I told you!" Teri said triumphantly.

"Told me what?" Claire asked, rubbing her forehead uneasily.

"You didn't read the paper?" Teri asked, pouncing.

Claire took the phone away from her ear, dangling it loosely in her left hand by her thigh. She stared across the room toward the kitchen and ended the call while Teri was still talking.

Claire set the phone on the living room table. The *Jaws* theme started to play over and over again as she walked slowly back into the kitchen.

She picked the paper up again and began turning the pages, carefully scanning each section. About six pages deep, among the Local News headlines, she saw it.

> ## CORONER SUSPECTS HOMICIDE IN TRACK FATALITY
>
> Evidence suggests woman's body placed on tracks in cover-up attempt. Corpse said to have been frozen for several years.

Things were becoming clearer. Usually when a train hits a human body at a high rate of speed, the body is warm and will basically explode on impact, leaving behind a long trail of blood and body parts. This is one of the telltale signs of impact location; inspectors walk backward from where the train stops to where the blood starts to determine the point of collision.

In Christine's case, that didn't happen; her body was stuck on the knuckle as though it had been speared. But it wasn't the sort of situation where your first thought would be, "Hey, this person should be in little pieces, what's up with that?" Still, it was making sense now. The body had been *frozen* and then *thawed* before being placed on the tracks. Christine's words began to resonate in Claire's mind. *This was what she had been 'waiting' for. She was directing me to the last owner of 421!*

"Holy shit!" Claire grabbed the phone, which was no longer ringing, though Teri had left her a voice mail. She dialed the St. Albans Police department and waited.

"Police," a man said in a slightly bored voice.

Claire began to feel uneasy, but she knew the spirit had been guiding her to this information. She was sure of it.

"Hi," she began, taking a deep breath. "I have a lead on the murderer in the track fatality case."

"Yes, ma'am." The officer immediately perked up. "And your name is?"

"Claire Montgomery," she responded matter-of-factly.

"Ms. Montgomery, we would love to hear any information that you may have. Is it possible for you to come down here to the station, or would you rather we send one of our detectives to you?"

Claire was quiet for a long moment. "We'll come to you."

She hung up and let out a long breath. She knew she had to call Teri. Her friend was often a difficult skeptic, but she would absolutely have her back.

"Hey," Teri said. "Are you okay? You hung up on me."

"Yes, I am fine," Claire replied, exhaling deeply. "I need you to come to the police station with me."

"For what?" Teri snapped, annoyance rising in her voice.

"You know exactly why," Claire shot back.

"Great," Teri sneered. "So now I'm going to go on the whack-job list, too?"

"You were the one that directed me to that article. Stop acting like you don't know something's going on here!"

There was a long pause.

"Are you picking me up?" Teri asked flatly.

"Yes. Be outside in ten."

"Roger that," came the reply, and the line went dead.

CHAPTER 9

JUST THE FACTS

Arriving at Teri's house, Claire didn't bother to go to the door. She sat in the car and waited.

Teri stepped out the front door a few minutes later, throwing her jacket on as she stomped to Claire's car. She wrenched the door open and flopped into the passenger seat with all her weight.

"Thanks for all the advance notice," Teri growled.

Claire tilted her head. "Were you eating raisins?"

"Oh, cripes," Teri said, rolling her eyes. "Are we really going to do the Scooby-Doo thing right now?"

They looked at one another, each feeling conflicted but for entirely different reasons.

"Teri, if you don't want to come, don't," Claire began, "but you do need to see what I have to deal with. This isn't some kind of joke. Talking to the police isn't something I consider fun. It's the last thing I wanted, but it's necessary at this point."

Teri looked down momentarily, covering her top lip with her bottom lip.

"Wellp," she began, slightly agitated, "Are you going to drive, or are we teleporting?"

Claire took a deep breath and shook her head as she put the car in drive.

They made the journey to the police station in silence. Teri looked out the window, periodically shaking her head in disapproval of...something. As they pulled into the parking lot, they were forced to weave around police vehicles that were scattered all over the lot; one was almost blocking the entrance.

Claire pulled into the closest vacant spot to the door. They looked at one another again as she turned the engine off and pulled the keys from the ignition. "Are you ready for this?" she asked.

"Sure," Teri shrugged. "It's your show." They got out of the car and walked through the double glass doors. Inside there was a short walkway leading to a counter. An officer looked up at them from behind a glass partition.

"Can I help you ladies?" He put on a flirtatious smile, his big brown eyes trying to swallow Claire whole.

"Yes," Claire replied. "I'm Claire Montgomery, I called a little while ago regarding the railroad case."

"Oh, yes!" he said, quickly leaning over and pushing a button on the wall next to him. As the loud buzzing noise made further conversation impossible, he simply pointed at a large steel door. Teri pushed it open and held it as Claire walked past her and into the hallway on the other side.

The tall, handsome officer was now standing in front of them.

"Right this way, ladies," he said as he turned and led them down a long hallway.

"Hubba, hubba," Teri muttered in Claire's ear as she followed behind her.

"Really?" Claire said, giving her friend a disdainful look. They weren't in Hops and Vines.

Teri just shrugged and laughed.

He left them in a large room that held several unoccupied desks. The room had a very masculine feel. Teri wasn't sure if that was because there wasn't a single plant around, nor one picture, or simply because their police department's staff was entirely male.

An olive-skinned man with salt-and-pepper hair slowly came out from behind a door that housed a private office. Somewhere in his forties, Claire guessed.

She stuck her hand out as he approached. "Hi," she said softly. "Claire Montgomery."

He took her hand with a firm grip, while searching her eyes in that way cops had— friendliness always tempered by suspicion. "Hi. Detective Tony Bellissimo," he said warmly. "The sergeant that took your call said you feel you have information to offer regarding the railroad case, is that true?"

Claire thought she could smell a cheap cigar but the Aqua Velva was too strong for her to be sure. "Yes, it is," she replied, glancing at Teri, who was looking at something apparently caught in her fingernail.

She glanced up. "Oh...yeah, hi...I'm Teri."

"Right this way," Bellissimo said, motioning them into his office.

Claire and Teri entered, and he closed the door gently behind them, but didn't lock it, which Claire found mildly reassuring. They could still make a break for it. There were two cushioned chairs opposite his desk, and they sat as Bellissimo perched on the corner of his desk in front of them, his arms folded loosely across his thick chest.

Teri glanced back and forth as the detective and Claire sat looking at one another in silence. After a few seconds, she elbowed her friend in the side. "This isn't an AA meeting; I think it's okay for you to just start talking."

"You need to look up someone named Doug," Claire blurted. "I don't know his last name, but there will be someone named Doug that Christine knew intimately."

The detective's face remained expressionless.

"Christine is the girl who was hit by the train. Doug is the person who killed her and put her on the tracks. I know it sounds crazy, but I am a road foreman and was the railroad official at the scene the night she was hit. She came to me when I was in the cab, downloading the data for my report."

"She came to you *after* she was hit?" Bellissimo asked, raising one eyebrow. Teri winced.

"Do you know what a medium is?" Claire asked him.

"Oh boy, here we friggin' go," Teri grumbled.

"Knock it off," Claire said, glaring at her.

"Yes, actually I do," he replied with a brief nod.

"Well, without getting too deep into it, that's what I am and yes, Christine's spirit appeared to me after she was hit by the train."

The detective gripped his bottom lip between thumb and forefinger. Claire looked angrily at Teri, who sat up straighter in her chair.

"So, to make sure I have this right...You want me to expend manpower and overtime hunting down some guy with only a first name, because you heard voices," Bellissimo said sarcastically.

"She didn't say she heard voices, she said the girl's spirit spoke to her," Teri snapped.

Claire smiled at her friend, then turned her attention back to the detective. "I'm trying to *save* you money, actually, by telling you this. My mental health is fine," she said, though no one had asked.

"Look ma'am, no offense, if the name Doug ever pops up I'll be sure to take a look, but that's the best I can do."

Teri could feel indignation coming off her friend in waves. Claire looked at her and nodded emphatically. "C'mon, we're done here."

The two women stood up. As Claire opened the door, she turned around. "By the way, detective. That voice I was hearing, after she was *dead*, had a thick accent. My best guess would be Russian." She winked at him and she and Teri walked out of the office and back down the hall. The detective stood motionless, watching them.

As they disappeared from view, he reached into his pocket and pulled out a small antique pocketknife. He'd carried it with him ever since his father passed away when he was just a boy. *Bullshit*, he thought. "Right, Dad?" he asked aloud, looking up toward the ceiling and sarcastically putting his hand to his ear. The room was silent. He laughed, shook his head, and dropped the knife back into his pocket.

"Sell that shit somewhere else, lady," he grumbled and closed the office door.

* * *

"I see what you mean," Teri said, slumping into the passenger seat of Claire's car without making eye contact.

Claire adjusted her seat belt in silence.

"Ya know," Teri began, "I just...I don't know, I guess it's just easier without the whole, 'what if?' aspect of death—to me, anyway."

"I understand," Claire replied softly.

"That pissed me off," Teri grumbled. "I didn't like the way he spoke to you."

"That's why I brought you," Claire said with a wink as she started the coupe. "To get pissed off on my behalf."

Teri laughed. "Got me figured out, eh?"

"A little," Claire replied as she adjusted the rearview mirror and put the car into drive.

"He did have a pretty nice...waist," Teri said sheepishly.

Claire started laughing. "Is that all you ever think about?"

Teri laughed as she took out a cigarette and lit it. "Kinda," she replied, rolling down the window and blowing the smoke out.

* * *

Detective Bellisimo drummed his fingers on the top of his desk uneasily. He opened his desk drawer and reached all the way to the back. He carefully pulled out an envelope with the words Christmas Money written across the front. He rubbed his fingers over the letters, then shoved it back into the drawer. "There's no way," he said, shaking his head as he got up from the desk.

* * *

Claire's phone rang. Teri picked it up and glanced at the screen. "Restricted," she said. "Do you want me to answer it?"

"I got it," Claire said, accepting the call and pressing the speaker button. "Hello?" she asked as she rounded a curve.

"Hi," the subdued male voice replied. "Is this Claire?"

"No, it's the friggin' Easter bunny," Teri grumbled, flicking ashes out the window.

"Yes, this is she."

Silence. Teri and Claire both looked at the phone, waiting.

"This is Detective Bellissimo," he began. "Look...I was rude and I apologize," he said solemnly.

Claire nodded. "It's all right," she said as they continued down the mountain. "I understand how it sounds."

"I need to tell you something and then I need you to answer my question, is that okay?" he asked.

"Sure," Claire responded casually.

"The girl who was hit by the train, Christine," he began, "she was Czech. How did you know that?"

Claire kept her eyes focused on the road beyond the windshield, and paused a moment before answering.

"How do you know that you are going to wake up in the morning?" she asked.

"I don't," he replied matter-of-factly.

"It's the same kind of thing, Detective. I don't know where it comes from, but it comes, and then I have to deal with it."

"Can I speak with you about this again next week?" he asked.

Teri glanced over at her. Claire rolled her eyes.

"Yes, Detective, but the second you start treating me like you are testing me, it ends."

"Got you," he said. "So I will call you next week then? Coffee, maybe?"

"Sure." Claire ended the call and dropped the phone back onto the console.

"What was that about? He wants to use you as the Psychic Network part of the investigation?" Teri laughed as she turned on the radio.

"Something like that," Claire said. Teri stared out the passenger side window so her smirk wouldn't be visible.

"I can't believe he told me he knew what a medium is and then acts like a jerk," Claire continued. "He probably only knows what he's seen on some dumb reality TV show." She glanced at Teri, who reached out to turn down the radio.

"I know that you believe in this stuff," she began, "and usually you're right when you toss out bits of insight or you blurt things that you couldn't possibly know. But there is no way a person who works in law enforcement is going to believe you. Claire, he just made you spill your guts and then basically told you to go screw yourself. You hit on a key point, and he's interested in how you knew that. But he's just stringing you along. He probably thinks you're cute and wants a reason to call you again."

"Why would I pretend to know something I don't? That isn't me at all. I take the spirit world seriously," Claire said, her voice rising.

"I know you do, but c'mon, you really think he is going to be looking for a guy named Doug? I don't think so," Teri said, waving her non-cigarette hand dismissively.

"Well, I know what I know. I know that Christine gave me that information because there is a lot more to the story than getting hit by a train. I never would have taken a chance going to the police if I didn't know with every fiber of my being that I needed to pass on that information," Claire said, beginning to doubt that it would help at all now.

"Can of worms," Teri said, raising her eyebrows as she flicked her cigarette butt out the window.

"Maybe," Claire replied with a shrug as she pulled into Teri's driveway. "Thanks for coming with me anyway."

"No problem," Teri said as she climbed out of the car. She turned around and leaned in the window to wink at Claire. "Burn a shrub or something and bring me some good luck."

"Asshole," Claire grinned as Teri jogged to her front porch.

* * *

As Claire opened her own front door, she kept thinking about their conversation. Teri already knew that other people didn't see things the way Claire did.

She slipped off her boots and hung her jacket behind the door. Teri was a complex person who liked to hide behind a tough exterior. Claire knew that she had gone through some difficult things to build that kind of crust. Teri never wanted to share the details, but the results were obvious.

Running her fingers through her hair as she passed into her living room, Claire felt certain that Teri would come to realize that it was okay to trust her. They had already invested a great deal of time into each other, and Claire was almost as stubborn as her friend.

Different scenarios began to play in her mind as she started the shower. *Will she ever stop thinking this is a joke? Is she capable of understanding that there is more out there? Is my best friend just an asshole?* The questions didn't stop, and Claire knew there was a reason behind Teri's resistance, but without her friend opening up to her, she couldn't figure out what it was.

She turned off the water and reached out of the tub to grab a towel from the basket nearby. As she wrapped it around herself, she wondered how she could ever fully introduce Teri to her world.

She headed into her bedroom, where she pulled on a sweatshirt and sweatpants. She still couldn't believe that she had a best friend who understood nothing about this part of her.

Walking to the kitchen, she poured herself a glass of milk and picked the newspaper up off the counter. Turning to the lifestyle/entertainment section, she looked to see what was going on over the weekend.

Karen Opal's name popped out at her immediately. There was going to be a benefit tomorrow for firefighters and Karen was hosting a message circle for it. *Maybe this is it*, she thought, and closed the paper.

CHAPTER 10

Messages From the Other Side

"Claire, where the hell are we going?" Teri asked as they pulled into the parking lot of the local volunteer firehouse.

"Don't worry, you'll love it," Claire said with a wide smile. "We are going to a benefit for the volunteer fire department. They have an amazing medium conducting a message circle."

"Medium! Message circle! You know I don't like that shit," Teri replied in an annoyed growl.

"I know, but it only lasts an hour and a half, and it's for a great cause. I really want you to see how clear the messages from the spirit world can be," Claire said as she parked near the rear of the lot.

"I'm not interested. I'm serious, I'm not, and if this is as much bullshit as I think it is, I am walking out." Teri slammed the car door shut, glaring at Claire.

"I get it, you're pissed. Look, we will find seats in the back, by the door. If you're really, really adamant about leaving after half an hour, I promise we can go. Hell, if we leave early, I'll buy dinner and the first round," Claire offered, hurrying to catch up to her friend.

The scent of fresh baked cookies and cocoa filled the air. The other side was just as anxious.

Once inside the firehouse, they looked around for two empty seats together. They found some on the far side of the room. On the way there, Teri looked around and counted close to eighty people in the room. She could tell that some were families, and thought others must be groups of friends. A lot of them were probably as skeptical as she was—at least she hoped so. She was also surprised to find that there were almost as many men as women.

"You have got to be kidding me. Men come for this crap too?" she said mockingly, as she draped her bomber jacket over the back of the metal chair.

"Yup. They want to hear from their loved ones, too," Claire said as she plunked down beside her. She laid her long black coat over her lap and made herself comfortable. She was surprised by the quick head snap Teri sent her way.

"Really, Claire? You're wearing a black top, black jeans, black shoes, and now you're covering your legs in your black coat. Is this some kind of Witch thing too?" Teri asked, only half-joking.

"Yes and no," Claire answered, straight-faced. "Witches can do mediumship, but it isn't the only thing they do. We do it all, from spells to rituals and even astral travel."

"Astral travel? You're killing me. You know I don't like this stuff, and yet you constantly want me to think about spells and rituals. I get it already, but what the hell is astral travel? Sounds like some seedy porn flick."

"Astral travel is not a seedy porn flick," Claire whispered patiently. "It's when you leave your body behind and go to another plane of existence. It's like taking a trip without your body. I don't do it so well, that is why mediumship interests me so much."

"I think I did that by accident once, when I was stuck in a really long line at the bank," Teri snarked. Just then, Karen Opal, the medium, walked to the front of the room. She had long, flowing dark hair, fair freckled skin and sported a big smile.

"I would like to begin by welcoming all of you," she said in a friendly, mellifluous voice. "It's wonderful to see such a large group of people out here in support of such a noble cause. Now, if you would all please take a moment to power off your cell phones, we can begin. We don't want to be interrupted by ringtones in the middle of a spirit's important message to their loved ones."

As Karen waited, the room rumbled with the sound of people rummaging around to turn off their phones. Moments later, it was quiet again.

Karen introduced herself and then gave a brief synopsis of her life and experiences, describing how she came from a long line of mediums and eventually turned her talents into a full-time job, doing the work she loved with spirits. She also explained that the lights would soon be turned down, at which point she would lead a ten-minute meditation to calm some people's nerves, and to get others relaxed enough that they would be open to hearing spirit messages.

"Just so you know, there are a lot of you here, and with limited time, some of the messages may cross, to hit more than one person or group of people at a time, so more messages can be delivered. Also, the seats you are sitting in are the perfect seats for you. There are no coincidences! You could be seated next to someone who needs to hear the same thing, and so the spirits may work together to bring you validation, peace, and some insight on a situation that you may not have even told anyone else about. I ask that you listen with a loving heart," she concluded. By now the room was filled to capacity—one hundred and fifty people.

With the lights dimmed, Karen turned on soothing background music and began the meditation. Claire, having some experience with these types of circles, knew it was designed to help raise the vibration of the room.

Karen began to give instructions in an even and relaxed tone. "Relax and sit upright in your chair with your palms up in the receiving position," she told the crowd. "Close your eyes and take a deep breath and release it with an *eeeeh*. Take another deep breath and release with an *aaaah*. And now one more, with an *ooooh*.

"Imagine you are deep within a forest and come upon a clearing filled with soft grass. You sit down and notice how soft the grass is and how wonderful it feels. It is a beautiful place that would be the perfect spot to speak with loved ones and friends that have passed from this world. Now imagine a loved one walking toward this spot of grass. They come to sit with you and smile. The smile is so warm and loving. It is your turn to talk with them. Ask them anything you would like. I will be back to get you in just a little bit."

Karen set the microphone down. The entire room remained quiet for about seven minutes, and then she spoke again.

"It is now time for your visit to end," Karen cooed. "Please say goodbye at this time. Now imagine standing back up and walking back in the direction you came. You start to notice that you are walking out of the forest and back to more familiar surroundings and you feel your body now back in the chair. You can now open your eyes."

Claire opened her eyes, wanting a message from her mom, but she also sensed that there were scores of spirits present, and that they were clamoring to give messages to their loved ones. She knew her mom would never take away someone else's chance to hear from a loved one, especially someone who didn't know for sure that the spirits were with them—and Claire certainly knew.

With the lights still dimmed, Karen approached a young woman in her twenties, seated a few rows from Claire and Teri. She was with two people who looked like they were her parents. Karen started talking about how there was a man in a leather jacket with a beard and big smile. She then looked right at the girl and said, "Your husband is so sorry that he never got to come home to you. He said that the accident was fast and that it didn't hurt. He was just surprised when the car crossed lanes and there was no place he could go."

Even in the dim light, the tears that flowed down the girl's cheeks were clearly visible. Karen continued, pointing out the necklace that the girl wore around her neck and how happy her husband was that she carried his ashes around with her. She acknowledged the girl's parents by sharing that her husband was glad she had moved back in with them and that he knew brighter days were ahead for her.

The communication was over. Karen glanced around the room, and walked all the way to the opposite side to talk to a man in his 60's.

"I have a 17 year-old male here and he says that he passed many years ago," Karen said and then began speaking to the older man directly. "This one here is a smart aleck!" Karen exclaimed. "He was definitely filled with a sense of humor and he wants you to know that there is no reason for you to be sad about his death. He tells me that you and your wife just celebrated your thirtieth wedding anniversary and that he loved the party. He said he was there for your wedding, too."

Karen started to laugh. "He's showing me a big top hat and asks if you swept out any chimneys on your way to get married?"

The whole firehouse erupted in laughter along with the older gentleman, whose long-dead brother had apparently just cracked a joke.

The man spoke, his voice breaking. "I always missed having him around. I was only 13 when he passed, and it left such a huge hole. Thank you." He wiped his eyes.

Claire looked at Teri and knew that they wouldn't be sneaking out. Teri had a half a sneer on her face, and was obviously searching for a tell or a flaw in the presentation. Eventually, Claire was sure she'd latch onto something that would allow her to chalk everything up to Karen's having planted people in the audience.

Shortly before the circle was due to end, Karen walked toward their section.

"I have a message here from a mother that died of lung cancer. I think it belongs here in this row," she said as she pointed to the row ahead of them.

Claire could see the look in Teri's eyes. Teri had lost her mom to lung cancer thirteen years earlier, and even through her suspicions, part of her was undoubtedly hoping this spirit was trying to reach her.

Karen kept giving evidence to the woman just ahead of them. She mentioned that the woman was Italian, that she liked to cook, that whoopie pies were the treat she would make every 4th of July.

With each piece of evidence, the woman ahead of them kept nodding her head more and more excitedly. But Teri was nodding slightly too.

Claire looked over at her friend and could see an orb of light hovering just over her left shoulder. She knew it was Teri's mom, and that the messages were piggy-backed.

Karen provided one last detail, about soft-pink pedal pushers that the woman had worn all summer long.

That was it. Game over. The look of wonder vanished from Teri's face, replaced with a grimace. "I knew this was all crap," she said as they were walking out.

"Come on, Teri, Karen talked about piggy-backing messages. You don't think it was your mom sending you a message, even with all the evidence that was exactly the same as she gave for the lady in front of us?" Claire pressed.

"Hell no. It was just throwing spaghetti at the wall to see what'll stick," the other woman shot back.

"You heard Karen. There are no coincidences, and she made mention that the seating arrange-ments were by design of the spirit world," Claire reminded, still trying to make even a tiny crack in the wall Teri had put up.

Unlocking the car, Claire watched as Teri sank into the passenger seat, sulking.

The ride to Hops and Vines was a quiet one. Claire asked Teri if she still wanted dinner.

"Yes, and I want that beer, too," Teri replied matter-of-factly.

"Okay, you're on!" Claire said and opened the car door.

Walking toward the entrance, Teri looked into Claire's eyes. "Do you think it really was my mother?" she asked, in an unusually subdued and thoughtful voice that was almost girlish. They stopped in the middle of the sidewalk for a mo-ment, and Teri held Claire's gaze, caught between defiance and hope.

"Yes, I do," Claire replied flatly, and walked past her friend and into the bar.

CHAPTER 11

UNCOMMON GROUND

Claire pushed her glasses down the bridge of her nose and watched Teri turn on her heel and stagger toward the ladies' room. *She's had enough.*

Looking down the length of the horseshoe-shaped mahogany bar, she caught Colleen's attention and waved her over. The stout redhead quickly maneuvered through the crowd. "Ready for another round?" she asked Claire with a mischievous smile.

"No," Claire replied quickly. "Would love a check though. I'm not sure what's gotten into Teri, but it's time to take her home."

Colleen giggled and excuse-me'd her way over to the register. Claire glanced toward the ladies' room again as the waitress returned.

"Here you go," she said, placing the tab on the wood and turning to walk away.

"Wait," Claire said, reaching out and touching Colleen's arm. "I want to get this settled up now, before she comes back and tries to order another one."

"Got ya," Colleen said with a wink as Claire pulled three twenties from her wallet.

"All set," Claire said, handing her back the tab and the cash. "Thank you."

"It's always nice to see you!" Colleen replied with a quick glance toward the ladies' room. Teri was lumbering back toward them. "And Teri too!"

They were still chatting as Teri finally returned.

"Where'd my drink go?" Teri asked, looking around suspiciously.

"Oh, I'm sorry, Claire said you guys were leaving." Colleen said, with a glance at Claire.

"Well, there's a glimpse into the future I didn't anticipate," Teri slurred. "Nah, I'm getting another one."

"No, you're not," Claire said sternly. "My day starts early tomorrow. I need to get home."

"You and your club sodas," Teri huffed.

Claire grabbed Teri's jacket from the barstool and held it out for her while her friend struggled to get her arms into the sleeves.

Although it was eleven o'clock on a weeknight, there was still a decent crowd in Hops and Vines. Teri, being a "regular," knew quite a few of the patrons. On her way to the door, she made sure to give every person a hug as though it had been her birthday party. The new waiter was no match for her, and turned crimson when the peck Teri had meant for his cheek landed squarely on his lips due to his squirming.

"Goodbye, everyone!" she called from the doorway as Claire shoved her out into the frigid night air.

Claire had hoped that the freezing temperatures would speed up Teri's pace, but no such luck.

"Hey," she said, as she stopped walking and stared at Claire's back. Claire rolled her eyes and turned to face her. The street was cold and quiet. "How did she know?"

"What are you talking about?" Claire asked, annoyed and ready to start physically dragging Teri to the car.

"How did that lady know so much about my mom, even though she was talking to the lady in front of us?"

"I told you," Claire began, grabbing Teri's arm and pulling her to get moving again. "Spirits will piggyback on messages to reach as many people as possible."

"Yeah, but it was my mom," Teri said, shaking her head.

"C'mon," Claire said softly, taking her by the arm again as she opened the car's passenger door. "Get in and warm up, we can talk on the way home."

Claire rushed around the car and jumped in, rubbing her hands together.

"Put your seatbelt on," she said. Teri was silent and still, and a single slow tear was sliding down her cheek. Claire knew that the alcohol was playing a part, but she also knew that Teri had needed to hear from her mother.

Teri was a tough cookie, but in the years following her mother's death, she'd been having a harder and harder time letting certain things go. She was self-protective and secretive, so Claire had been forced to piece together a picture of her friend's life using only the fragments of information Teri would reveal during those rare moments that her guard wasn't up.

She knew that Teri's parents had been extremely strict. She also knew that Teri had had an abortion at 14, but would never talk about it in any detail.

Claire believed that it had something to with the religious cult she'd been forced into by her parents. Some Jim Jones type had gotten into her mother and father's heads and, next thing you know, Teri was pregnant. That was her assumption, anyway.

They were close enough that Teri had told her that much; Claire respected her friend's silence, and never delved beyond whatever Teri would offer.

What she was sure of was that Teri's mom wanted to pass a message to her daughter that she was still with her and that she loved her very much.

"C'mon," Claire said, reaching over and buckling Teri's seatbelt for her. "Let's get you home."

Teri nodded and turned to gaze out the window, swiping at her cheek with one hand.

Claire eased out of the parking lot and headed to the west side of town where Teri lived.

It had been quiet for a while. Claire glanced over at Teri. She knew she was troubled.

"Do you doubt that you are alive?" Claire asked.

Teri looked over at her, puzzled. "No."

"Do you know why you're alive?" Claire prodded.

"Don't start this crap again. I can't take it right now," Teri snapped.

"If you are alive, and you accept that fact without any kind of reason, then why is it so hard to believe that there are other levels of existence?"

"Fine, maybe," Teri said with a shrug. "I don't know anymore."

Claire pulled into the driveway of Teri's house. It was the same one in which she'd grown up. Her parents had moved out of state with the cult, and Teri had chosen to stay in the house, which said more to Claire about her friend than she'd ever admit.

Claire parked and trotted around the car to Teri's side. She opened the door, unlocked the seatbelt, and helped her out of the car.

The walkway was still covered with powdery snow from two days earlier. Their feet created small white clouds as they walked to the front door.

"Where are your keys?" Claire asked, grabbing at the sides of Teri's bomber jacket as her friend swayed back and forth. "Got 'em," she said with a sigh, fishing a keyring worthy of a janitor from Teri's pocket.

"It's the pink one," Teri said with a soft burp.

Pushing the door open, they were greeted by Teri's long-established lack of interest in housekeeping.

"You have to get your shit together, lady," Claire said, shaking her head and smiling.

"Yeah, probably," Teri said with a shrug.

Claire wasn't sure if it was the frigid air or the emotions Teri was going through, but she noticed that the other woman was no longer staggering, and seemed quite clearheaded. Claire gave her a hug and promised to call her in the morning.

She walked out of the house, closing the door gently behind her, and grabbed the shovel that was propped against the house. With quick, forceful strokes, she pushed the light, fluffy snow out of the way. As she returned the shovel to its place on the porch and turned to walk toward her car, the front door flew open and Teri came flying out of the house.

"Ha ha!" she yelled as she tackled Claire into the snow. Both giggling and out of breath, the friends stretched out their arms and legs, swinging them back and forth and making a pair of perfect snow angels on the lawn.

"What the hell am I going to do with you?" Claire laughed, as they both stood up and brushed themselves off.

"Who knows," Teri said over her shoulder as she jogged back inside and slammed the door behind her.

Claire got back into the car grinning.

CHAPTER 12

HELLO AGAIN

At eight o'clock the next morning, Claire's phone began to ring. She gently lifted Coal off of her chest, setting her on the bed beside her, and then grabbed the phone from the nightstand.

"Hello?" she answered groggily.

"Hi, Claire. I hope I didn't wake you?" It was Detective Bellissimo.

She sat up in bed. "No, it's fine," she answered. "What can I do for you, detective?"

"I really need to talk to you." He hesitated for a moment. "About the case."

"Okay," Claire responded. "What do you want to know?"

"Can we meet for a coffee, or breakfast or something?" he asked.

"Sure," Claire said, looking at the clock on the wall.

"Can I pick you up at your place in an hour, or...?"

"Yes. That will be fine." She thought for a second. "How do you know where I live?"

"I'm a detective," he replied with a chuckle.

"Okay." Claire thought it was more like the behavior of a stalker than a detective. Before he could reply, she ended the call.

Bellissimo frowned at the phone with amusement, and put it in his pocket.

Claire had a jittery feeling, but she wasn't sure what it was about. She shook it off, grabbed Coal, and walked to the kitchen to make a pot of coffee before taking a shower. She wanted to be as mentally prepared as possible, and being in control of her outer presentation would make her feel cool, calm, and in control. This was a technique that she often needed to employ, and one that worked well for her.

Exactly one hour later, a soft knock came at her door, and she knew that it was Bellissimo. She flipped her hair back as she left the kitchen to answer it.

"Hi," Bellissimo said with a grin as she opened the door. She was more conscious of his looks than she'd been on their first meeting, when she'd been focused on getting him to take her seriously about Doug and the murder. Now she noticed his high, rough cheekbones and his muscular build. *Kinda Rocky meets Al Pacino in the eighties,* she thought, returning his smile and stepping aside to allow him in.

"Hi. Come in," she said, nudging away Coal, who was already trying to get his attention.

The detective followed her silently into the kitchen.

"I thought we'd go to Kirk's Diner," he offered.

"No point. Have a seat," she said, waving at the table, where two plates were already laid out. He sat.

"Coffee?" she asked.

"Sure, if you're having one."

"Yep," she replied with a smile and poured him a cup.

"So," he began as he grabbed the sweetener and cream, "did you know Doug or Christine before the tragedy?"

"Nope," she replied flatly, sitting down opposite him and sipping her own coffee.

"There's a piece I can't fit here, Claire, I have to be honest." His large brown eyes bore down on her. "Christine had been printed for petty theft here in the states several years ago, when she was a kid. And those records revealed that she was missing from the Czech Republic." He sat quietly for a moment, staring into Claire's eyes. "There's no way you could have known she had an accent, nor her nationality, if you'd never met her before… it's bothering me."

Claire returned his gaze, betraying no emotion. "I can only tell you what I know, and what I know comes from what I heard, and what I heard comes from a place that you either cannot or will not accept exists."

His face darkened. He stood up and leaned across the table, looming over her.

"I'm not playing games here," he said in a rougher voice than before. But as angry as he sounded, she didn't feel threatened. Maybe it was because she was in her own kitchen, with sunlight filtering through canary yellow curtains, and not a harshly lit interrogation room, but the whole cop thing just didn't carry as much weight.

"How did you know her?" he asked again.

"Do you smoke?" Claire responded.

"No," he answered, annoyed.

"Yes you do," Claire insisted. "I can smell smoke under your cologne."

"What the hell are you talking about?" He threw his hands in the air. "I just said I don't fucking smoke. Why won't you just answer my question?"

She stood up, grabbed her cell from the countertop, and called Teri. Bellissimo waited, glaring at her.

"Yeah, what's up?" Teri answered.

"Hey," Claire said. "I've got this detective in my kitchen and he just doesn't get it."

"On my way," Teri said and immediately ended the call. Claire set the phone back on the counter, and she and the detective stood staring at one another in silence for more than ten minutes. Finally, he sat down, and out of courtesy, she did too.

"So," he began again. "You just knew she had an accent and was most likely Russian, that's what you want me to believe, is that right?"

"Yes," Claire answered calmly, just as Teri burst through the front door.

"Hey!" Teri yelled as she barreled into the kitchen. "Oh! Hi, Detective!" she said animatedly. Claire couldn't hide her grin; she knew her friend too well. "I thought I smelled donuts," she said with a smile, looking sheepishly at the detective.

"Human trafficking is serious," he said, looking at Teri and Claire with an expression like a middle school vice principal. "This isn't a joke," he grimaced.

"Human trafficking?" Claire asked.

He glared at her and stood up. He put his coffee cup in the sink, which she thought was nice of him, and walked toward the door.

"There's something wrong here. I'll figure it out. But the two of you better fucking hope you're not implicated in any way, or we're going to go round and round," he warned.

Teri and Claire were speechless, watching him storm out and slam the door behind him. After a moment, Teri looked at Claire, who was staring into her coffee mug. "Human trafficking? He's off his rocker," she said, picking at her ponytail.

Claire stared at her blankly for a moment as she absorbed the detective's words, and then grabbed her wool coat from the hallway. "Let's get out of here."

* * *

Claire and Teri sat together on a large boulder on the shoreline, staring at the frozen portion of the lake in front of them. The day was still, the air frigid, and the mood tense.

"We have to let this whole Christine thing go," Teri said bluntly and then took a sip of her coffee. She looked over at Claire.

"I know we do," Claire responded after a moment, tossing a small stone onto the ice, where it slid until it fell off the edge with a plunk. "I know we do."

"It's on the cops now," Teri said. "There's only so much you can do."

"I realize that," Claire said, taking a sip from her cup. "The human trafficking thing is what's bothering me. How many other girls are out there?"

"Of course it's bothering you, it's shitty and creepy and anything else you want to call it, but it's not our gig, Claire, we have to move on and let it go now," Teri replied pointedly.

"I know," Claire responded softly. "I just feel like..." She hesitated. "I don't know, I just feel like there's something missing."

"Yeah," Teri quipped, standing up. "A shot of tequila. Let's go."

Claire rolled her eyes. "I wish I had your gift of brushing shit off like it's nothing."

"It's not that it's nothing," Teri countered as they began to walk back up the hill. "It's something, but it's something we can't control, so let it go already." She shrugged.

CHAPTER 13

DEMON ON THE TRACKS

Claire was staring out the large café window after an early dinner with Teri at their favorite old-school Italian restaurant at the edge of town. She ran through all the spiritual drama she'd been subjected to over the last week.

Christine's murder and ghostly visitation had shaken her to the core. It had been nice to watch Karen bring comfort to the bereaved people in the firehouse, but Claire still had a best friend who didn't really believe, and with whom she was unable to share her world. She spent the majority of her time now, at least as far as Teri was concerned, focusing on their jobs with the railroad.

"I really don't want to go," Claire grumbled into her teacup.

"Knock it off and just do it," Teri said sharply.

Claire had been a road foreman for more than a year, but a few of the guys still gave her attitude. Steve was the worst. He had been on the railroad for more than thirty years and therefore thought he was "the cat's ass," as her father used to say. He didn't think a woman belonged on a train except as a passenger, never mind as his boss.

Steve's work record was dismal. He'd been held out of service several times, and had even been fired—twice. And yet, he was still there, which meant Claire was stuck trying to correct his train-handling skills while dealing with his shitty attitude on top of it. Tomorrow morning, it was his turn for a compliance ride.

As if dealing with him wasn't enough, Claire was also on edge because they would be going over the same track where Christine had been hit. It bothered her and left her with endless questions no one could answer—and Teri's sarcasm wasn't helping, either. She knew her friend meant well, but some things a person doesn't just get over. It was insulting.

Teri was glaring at her impatiently.

"Stop pushing me. I know I have to go," Claire snapped. Taking the last swig of her lukewarm tea, she knew that she couldn't put it off any longer.

She stood up from the table and began to gather her belongings for the trip. Suddenly, almost surprising herself, she bent down to give her friend a hug.

"Thanks. I needed a kick in the ass," Claire said, forcing a nervous smile. "That asshole just stresses me out. I'm constantly putting out the fires he starts, and then I hear about him bad-mouthing me left and right."

A grin spread across Teri's face. "You're not going to break out the cayenne pepper again, are ya?" she asked with a wink.

After all these years, it still pissed her off that Teri would never acknowledge a difference between protection and retribution in the Craft, no matter how painstakingly she tried to explain it. In Claire's view, no matter what you do or don't believe, you can't challenge the fundamentals of a person's faith, *particularly* if you don't know anything about the subject. But with Teri, it was the same every time: When Claire told her she was merely trying to protect herself from Steve's negative energy, and that anything that happened to him would be a direct result of his own assaults ricocheting back at him threefold, she refused to hear it, and mocked her for "cursing" her co-workers.

Claire rolled her eyes. "I'll call you when I am back from this ride from hell," she said and walked out to begin the drive to Alderon, the station from which the compliance ride would depart.

Alone in the car, she kept her energy up on the road through the mountains by listening to her favorite band, Shinedown. Suddenly thinking of Christine, she turned up the volume.

"Sometimes goodbye—is a second chance," she sang.

Passing Otter Creek, the halfway point between St. Albans and Alderon, she turned the stereo off. She drove in silence, mentally preparing for the challenging trip she would be taking in the morning.

In her head, Claire was going over the physical characteristics of the railroad between St. Albans and Alderon, Vermont. She visualized every curve and speed restriction, along with all the other cues that signaled upcoming mile markers and stations. Knowing every section of the track was important. The details needed to be fresh in her mind before she climbed onto the engine to evaluate Steve's train-handling skills. After all, in the worst-case scenario, she might have to take control herself.

She'd been "out of the seat" on a regular basis, which would make it easy to get sloppy. With someone like Steve, she couldn't risk it.

The drive over the almost-deserted highway was over before she knew it. Grabbing her backpack, Claire walked into to the lobby of the local Molibur Inn.

"Hey, Claire," the front-desk clerk called before she even reached the counter. Even though she hadn't been there in quite some time, she thought it was nice that Melissa remembered her.

Melissa started tapping on the keyboard. "I saw your name on the list, and I am putting you in your favorite room—on the first floor, near the pool," she said with a big smile.

After exchanging pleasantries with Melissa, Claire took the key and headed for the room. She set her bag on the bed and pulled out her bathing suit. There was just enough time to get in a few laps before the crew from the northbound train were due in. She wasn't eager to run into them.

The sharp chlorine smell struck her nostrils even before Claire opened the door to the pool. The promise of the warm water was so inviting that she ignored the NO JUMPING sign and plunged into the deep end. Her plan was to relax after the drive and hopefully tire herself out by doing laps so she would fall asleep quickly. She didn't want to lay awake thinking about Christine, or that asshole Steve.

Twenty-five minutes later, still dripping wet, Claire wrapped the white towel around her waist and walked back to her room. After drying off, she slipped between the covers. It was still early, but the exercise had done the trick, and she drifted off to sleep.

* * *

Claire used her least favorite sound—quacking ducks—as her phone's alarm; it woke her up just before six AM. She had a quick breakfast in the lobby, still wearing the sweats she'd slept in. Afterward, she returned to her room to prepare for the long day ahead.

She wanted to present the strongest front possible, so there would be no bullshit from the crew. She dressed in thick blue jeans, a military green sweater, and heavy black, steel-toed work boots. She tried to de-emphasize her scar with makeup, but wound up putting on too much and had to scrub it all off, turning her eyes puffy and red in the process. Oh, well. She shook her head and returned to the lobby to meet up with the crew.

She was the first to arrive, and set her work bag on the floor near the oversized fireplace.

"Why are you here? Taking the train for a spin?" Skip, the contracted taxi driver, mumbled at her through a mouthful of jelly donut.

Claire was about to answer when the elevator doors opened. Steve stalked out and stood facing her.

"You coming with me?" he growled.

"Yes, I am," Claire replied stoically, resting her palm over the scar.

"Fine. Skip, let's go, I'm not eating with her. Bring me to the diner," Steve ordered and stormed past her to the taxi waiting outside.

"He really likes you, huh?" Skip said sarcastically as he walked out behind Steve.

"Guess I'm driving myself," Claire muttered under her breath. She was grateful for the last precious moments of solitude, frankly. Grabbing her work bag, she drove the five miles to the tiny station.

Claire parked behind the building and for the first time in weeks, called on her spirit guides. "Keep me safe, guys, today is going to be a doozy," she implored as she opened the car door.

Out of nowhere, a gust of wind slammed her door shut, missing her fingers by inches. She tried to open it again, but it wouldn't budge. She tried several times, even ramming into it with her left shoulder; nothing. She stopped and sat back in the seat, looking quizzically at it for a moment, and then gently tried one more time. It opened with ease, as if it had suddenly been unlocked. Stepping outside, she took note that there was no more than a slight breeze in the air.

Grimacing, she grabbed her work bag and crossed from the parking lot to the back entrance, walking through the station's waiting room to the crew room. She was the first to arrive, again, and sighed with relief, thinking she would have a few minutes to grab all of her bulletins and get her paperwork up to date in peace. Moments later, though, the door slammed against the wall as the crew arrived.

She watched as Frank followed Steve into the room. It was bad enough that she had to carry around the thought of Christine. Now Frank, the conductor on the train that had hit her, would be another reminder. She took a deep breath and sat down across from them at the small picnic table inside the crew room.

They held a job briefing, and every line on each bulletin was gone over in great detail. Claire knew this extra-thorough briefing was a show for her benefit, as both Frank and Steve were more than uncomfortable having her there.

Briefing complete, they filed out and approached the waiting train. The sun was shining and ice sparkled in the tree branches like dancing diamonds. It was a beautiful day for a train ride. *Too bad it has to be with Steve,* Claire thought as she walked down the platform toward the engine.

Climbing up the ladder and placing her work bag on the middle seat, she grabbed the paperwork and verified that all of the required mechanical tests had been performed.

She knew the paperwork would be perfect and up to date. The mechanical crew up here was always on their A game; it was the one place she never had to worry about.

She could hear Steve yelling something snide back to Frank, and then the door to the engine flew open. Steve threw his work bag up through the door and onto the floor of the cab as he reached the top step.

As he entered, she noticed how short he was and wondered if that had something to do with his negative attitude. *Napoleon Syndrome*, she thought. She would have to look it up later.

"Okay, Steve, let's get on the same page here and get this train over the road," Claire said, cheerful but firm.

Steve grabbed the reverser, pushing it to the forward position, and then knocked off the brakes to build up the air pressure as he prepared for the required pre-departure brake test.

"Okay to set 'em up," came Frank's command over the radio.

"Setting them up," Steve replied.

"Okay to release."

"Here comes the release."

"Good class two, complete with marker," Frank concluded, ending the transmission.

"Good on the brakes, good marker," Steve parroted back, still holding the mic.

"Okay to depart Alderon," the crackling voice said as it cut through the silence of the cab.

"Departing Alderon on time. How many on board?" Steve asked.

"We got nine," Frank replied.

"Okay, thanks," Steve said. Glaring at Claire for a moment, he lifted the handset again and said, "Out."

Yup, this is going to be one hell of a day, Claire thought as she began filling out the blanks on the Federal Railroad Administration evaluation sheet. She needed to make sure that she made all of the required observations, and those that were not going to be made on this trip needed to be discussed to make sure Steve understood them.

The engine crested the top of a hill near a dairy farm, and Claire noticed how beautifully the snow- and ice-covered trees on either side of the tracks seemed to meld together, creating a magical-looking archway over the tracks. The fullness of the snow disguised the fact that they were only about thirty feet from one of the main roads.

If any engineer other than Steve was here, this would be a perfect day, Claire thought as she glanced at her wristwatch. They were an hour into their trip, and six minutes outside their next stop, and he hadn't spoken a word to her. *Perfect.*

As they rounded the curve, the train whizzing down the hill toward the next town, something ahead caught Steve and Claire's eyes at about the same time. There was a figure on the tracks.

Steve reacted instantly, placing the train into emergency mode. The hissing of air and the sound of metal against metal grew to a shriek as the train, still traveling at more than ninety miles per hour, cannonballed toward the figure.

This can't be fucking happening again, Claire winced.

A few seconds before impact, the figure turned his head and looked up. Claire had learned from many interviews over the years that when a person gets hit by a train, from the engineer's perspective it always looks as if the trespasser is staring right at you. But they are actually looking at the headlights.

This time, however, Claire and Steve were able to see right into the person's eyes. They saw his face clearly just before he turned around and tucked his head. *He was smiling.*

The design of the engine obstructed the last fifteen feet prior to impact. Within less than a second, they heard the unmistakable *thump* and the crunching sound of bones being minced as they popped against the bottom of the train as it began to slow.

"Emergency! Emergency! Emergency! Train number 65 in emergency at mile post 312," Steve hollered into the mic.

"You guys okay up there?" Frank's voice over the radio was tense and fearful.

"Yeah, we are okay. We hit a guy standing in the gage. You are going to have to go a little more than a quarter of a mile back, Frank. I am going to tone up the dispatcher." Steve was running on autopilot, his voice a monotone.

Claire's arms suddenly began to tingle, and the hair on the back of her neck was rising. *Please!* she pleaded desperately in her mind. *Not now! Not in front of this asshole!*

A moment later she became nauseated as the smell entered her nostrils. She knew that smell. She began to scratch the scar on her cheek apprehensively as the most evil-sounding voice she'd ever heard growled in her ear and the temperature in the locomotive's cab began to drop.

Well, this guy doesn't seem to like you too much, now does he, Claire? the spirit sneered.

CHAPTER 14

DEAD MAN WALKING

Emergency crews from multiple agencies were filling the right of way near the tracks like a parade. A second track fatality in such a short time was the biggest thing to hit the area in years, and all available personnel were responding. Even off-duty officers and firefighters who had been listening to their scanners, or been called by colleagues, were parking on the main road and walking to the scene.

These incidents were never easy, and being with a prick like Steve wasn't helping. Claire's senses were heightened. The spirit had chosen not to show himself and was hiding, but she could feel his presence, dark and violent.

"What smells like shit?" Steve yelled, looking over at her with revulsion.

She cringed. *He's here*, she thought stiffly. The smell was putrid, like burnt hair and sulfur. They both began to gag as Steve threw open the window.

The heat had been going full blast, but the entire engine cab was frigid within seconds.

"Who is in charge here?" A man's voice boomed through the open window from the ground. "I am Officer Johnson with the Preston Police Department," he shouted.

Claire stuck her head out.

"I am. Road Foreman Montgomery, I am in charge of the train and crew," Claire replied robotically.

The spirit began to chuckle evilly. *You like to think so*, it muttered in her head.

"What happened?" the officer yelled up again. "All we see is a bunch of guts on the engine."

"You need to walk back," Claire yelled, ignoring the spirit. "There will be a large debris field on both sides of the tracks. There was a guy in the middle of the track. He saw us, but he didn't get out of the way."

Forcing herself to stay present and with the living, Claire focused her mind on the spirit for just a moment. *I absolutely cannot talk with you right now.*

Suddenly the lights inside the engine cab turned off in defiant response. The heaviness she felt in her chest told her this wasn't going to be good.

The constant communications between emergency personnel had the engine radio chirping every couple of seconds. Claire looked at Steve. "I'm going to go out to assist the police and answer any questions. I'll be back up once that's done," she told him.

Steve nodded dismissively without looking at her.

Donning her gloves and safety glasses, she walked to the back room of the engine and took a handful of paper towels and a trash bag from the crew pack. She opened the fireman's-side door and carefully descended the ladder, watching her footing and scanning the area for debris.

When a train hits a human being, the scene is gruesome to say the least. Brain matter, blood, and guts usually get strewn over at least a one-mile stretch of track. A road foreman assigned to investigate a fatality on the railroad cannot come into contact with any stray body fluids or parts; hence the gloves and paper towels. Those towels are then placed in a heavy-duty trash bag and sealed, after which the bag is taken away by the local biohazard team.

Claire reached the bottom of the ladder, relieved that the entity hadn't tossed her off the engine, and that the paper towels she held in her grip had nothing on them but dirt. She tossed them into the big black trash bag and started to walk toward the rear of the train, where she could see a large group of people standing around.

As she arrived, a side door opened on the last coach and Joe, the assistant conductor, looked out at her.

"Anything you want me to do, Claire?" he asked.

"Just keep the people informed and safe. If you need to, hand out some water," Claire said. She continued to walk, away from the train and toward the crowd milling around close by. The police were doing a good job keeping them away from the crew.

When Claire was within earshot of the police, she heard a small cheer go up.

What the hell are they cheering about? Claire asked herself, bewildered.

When she reached the group she identified herself and let the police know that she had also been on the locomotive with the engineer, if they had any questions.

"Thank you," a Vermont state trooper, an older man with a few wisps of white hair trailing across a huge bald spot, said with a grin.

"It's my job," Claire said matter-of-factly, trying to cover her scar with her hair. Meanwhile, members of the growing crowd were intermittently high-fiving each other as though they had just won the office lottery pool. Claire didn't know what the hell they had to be so happy about; uncomfortable, she stepped back a few feet.

"You did us a huge favor; that guy was scum," said an officer standing nearby. He was wearing a faded green uniform that was clearly too tight for his belly.

"I don't know what you are talking about," Claire replied, taken aback. "I really have no idea."

"That piece of shit opted to off himself because he couldn't face what he had done," said one of the guys from the middle of the group.

The trooper introduced himself as Telford Roy. "We found a note," he said. "A few of the guys read it before I got here. With the ID and a few other items we found, it was clearly a suicide."

"Yeah, he was a piece of shit!" shouted one of the firefighters.

"He was a pedophile," one of the other men chimed in. "He just got bailed out and was going to be tried next month for raping two Girl Scouts."

"What a shame he didn't suffer," a third voice scowled.

"That's enough," said Trooper Roy sternly. "Can't you see this poor woman has been through enough without you congratulating her? What the hell is the matter with you guys? Get back to your jobs, we need to clear this scene," he ordered.

With her head reeling and her stomach in knots, Claire struggled to stay professional and not scream at the whole gang of assholes who were busy "thanking" her.

Did they have any idea what it feels like to be in the cab of a locomotive when you hit someone?

She focused on answering all of the questions that were being lobbed at her by both Trooper Roy and the growing crowd. For example: *Can I see your license?* (Road foremen have a certificate they must carry when they run an engine.) *Will the trains still be running tomorrow? Is the engineer dead, too? Are we allowed to take pictures? Can I thank the engineer, that's the driver, right? Who's going to drive the train now?*

Claire noticed two troopers climbing up the side of the engine, where Steve was still sitting in the cab and rushed back toward them, but they were already inside before she got there.

Steve was starting to come unglued during the officers' questioning. His entire body was shaking, and his eyes were bloodshot. He seemed like he was about to start crying. It was the first time that Claire had ever seen him like that. She almost felt sympathetic.

"Have you been drinking anything today?" the officer asked.

"Okay, that's enough," Claire said, waving the officer away. It seemed Steve wasn't as tough as he tried to act, and the fact that he was losing it in front of the officers and Claire was something she wasn't prepared for.

"Wow, Steve, are you okay?" Claire asked, once the two officers had climbed back down and were out of earshot.

"I'm fine!" Steve said, with a venom that made Claire recoil a bit—and just when she had begun to feel sorry for him. Yes, these incidents were hard, but trying to pretend they didn't affect you was a terrible idea. *I never realized just how dysfunctional a human being Steve is,* Claire said to herself.

"It's a head! A head!" Frank's voice exploded from the radio with a clang of feedback. A chill raced through Claire's body. Steve bent over, cupping his face in his hands and rocking back and forth.

"Oh, no," Claire whispered. She opened the fireman's-side door and looked down.

Frank was standing at the bottom of the engine ladder looking up at her, blood covering his hands. A severed head sat on the ground next to him in the snow. Frank was grinning. Claire turned back toward the inside of the cab and began to gag, her eyes stinging with tears.

"What? What is it?" Steve yelled, terrified, as he got up from the seat and approached her.

She raised her head and stared at him with a steely gaze. "I am ordering you to sit your fucking ass down, right now," she said forcefully.

Steve lowered his eyes and slumped back into his seat.

Claire breathed heavily through her nose. She opened the door to the engine and began to climb down the ladder.

Before her feet touched the ground, Frank was mumbling at her, "He did it."

Claire let go of the ladder. Avoiding the ground, she looked at Frank instead. His mouth was twitching and he started scratching his scalp as though he were trying to get something off of him. "He's the one who did it! He did it! I didn't do it, he did it!" he yelled almost incoherently.

Claire stared at him. She wasn't sure if he was losing his mind or going into shock. She looked toward the front of the engine, waving Trooper Roy over. As he got closer, he spotted the head on the ground and called someone on his radio.

Claire stepped toward the trooper. "Officer, my conductor needs help, he's cracking up." Roy nodded and grabbed Frank gently around the shoulders, leading him away from the engine as emergency personnel approached, wearing rubber boots and gloves and carrying black bags.

Claire slowly climbed back up to the locomotive's cab. Steve hadn't moved. She sat across from him in silence. Without pulling her phone to check, it seemed to her that more than an hour had passed.

She picked up her portable radio. "Road Foreman Montgomery to Trooper Roy, over."

"Trooper Roy to Road Foreman Montgomery, the scene is clear, you are free to go. We've sent your conductor to St. Mary's hospital in St. Albans for evaluation, over."

The questions had been answered, the officers were now gone, the train had been released from their hold. They were now cleared to continue the trip to St. Albans. The relief crew had yet to arrive, though.

Claire pulled out her cell and told the crew manager to have them in place at St. Albans, that it would be best to get moving and that she would be taking control.

Steve was in no shape to complete the trip, which meant she was required to continue on as the engineer, taking the train down the road to a point where a relief engineer could take over. Although the incident had shaken her badly, she had enough knowledge of how the spirit world worked to understand that even after what had happened, what most people consider reality is just one of many.

"Head end to the assistant conductor, over," Claire called over the engine's radio mic.

"Conductor answering, over," Joe replied softly.

"We have been released, and Frank has been taken to the hospital. Can you come up here for a job briefing? I need you to take over as conductor."

"Heading up," Joe answered.

"Steve, I am sending you back to the coaches for the rest of the trip," she told the engineer, just before the door behind his seat opened and Joe climbed into the cab for the job briefing.

Claire looked at him. "Joe, you did a great job keeping the passengers informed and calm. I know that it has been a tough morning, so thank you for your help and agreeing to keep heading south to meet up with our relief crew."

Joe nodded at her solemnly.

"I know it isn't the usual circumstance, but this way we can get relief sooner by meeting them," Claire said, pausing to take a breath. "I think they got lost." She giggled a bit, breaking the tension.

Claire looked at Joe a moment and then paused. "Wow, Joe, you drink herbal tea?" she asked.

Joe stared at her as though she had grown a spare head. "Well a few hours ago I did have a chamomile tea, the coffee was nasty." He looked at her uneasily.

"We are going to take it nice and easy on the way south," she continued. "I am going to run the train and I am going to have Steve sit in the back with you. Any questions?"

"No, that sounds like a plan. Let's go over the bulletin again and then we can call the dispatcher and get permission to continue," Joe said.

With all of the necessary requirements met, Claire sat down in the engineer's seat, thankful she had taken the time on the ride up to go over the physical characteristics of the run.

After they inspected the train and then performed a class-two brake test, she waited for Joe to jump back on the train and button up.

"Okay to depart from where we stand, with track warrant number 643 to proceed from MP 312 to St. Albans, over," Joe's voice came over the radio.

"Okay to depart from where we stand, with track warrant number 643 to proceed from MP 312 to St. Albans," Claire repeated.

"Here we go," she said, and put the reverser into forward and slowly pulled out on the throttle.

The train started to move and Claire did a running brake test to make sure all the brakes were working properly. "Good on the running test," she called back to Joe.

Joe's response was barely audible as Claire became aware that she wasn't alone in the cab anymore.

Wow. Claire heard the low, evil growl in her mind. *They let you drive a train?*

"Okay, I don't have time to deal with you right now," Claire snapped, speaking aloud toward the presence that was now directly behind her. The smell had returned, too. "You need to go away. I'm busy."

You can hear me, I know you can, so listen to me very carefully. I am not going away, he snarled.

"Approaching Preston with track warrant number 643 to proceed to St. Albans, out," announced Claire, using the foot-pedal radio control.

Shifting her focus to running the train, she started blowing the horn for the three crossings coming up, gradually reducing the throttle notch, which reduces the power controlling the locomotive's speed, so she could start braking for the upcoming station stop.

"Four cars to go," Joe called over the radio. "Two cars. One. When you get 'em stopped it'll be far enough," he concluded.

The voice snarled at her again. *Do you think I stood in front of your train by accident? I read the paper by the way; sorry about Christine, she was a sweet little piece of ass when she was younger.*

"Okay to depart Preston," Joe called.

"Okay to depart Preston on track warrant number 643, with a proceed clearance to St. Albans, out," Claire replied, her voice lowering as she spoke each word.

The hair on her arms stood up. The ball of tension in her stomach was swelling, and the fact that this spirit was talking about Christine that way was making her skin crawl. Why was he doing this?

These thoughts played over and over in Claire's mind as she continued to head south at a slower-than-normal speed, scratching at her scar, hoping the relief crew would meet the train soon.

Focus, just focus, she commanded herself. *Get the job done and* then *try and figure out what the hell that was about.*

The foul stench suddenly disappeared and the temperature in the cab rose to a comfortable and steady seventy-four degrees. He was gone.

The conductor was doing a lot of talking on the radio, making sure to keep everyone on the same page. When Claire had first started, one of the older engineers had always talked about the conductor being the drum that carried the beat. She was finally able to understand what he meant.

Just outside the next stop, the faint calls from the trainmaster transporting the relief crew could be heard.

"We are here at the station ready to take over. Bring it in nice and slow, stop short of the south crossing," the trainmaster told her over the radio.

What a welcome sound, Claire thought. A wave of emotions swept over her as she brought the train to a stop in front of the St. Albans station as directed. She gathered her things and climbed down the ladder and walked across the parking lot to the waiting trainmaster's company vehicle.

The trainmaster opened the door for her and she climbed in. She wasn't about to make small talk. She closed her eyes and went over everything that had happened since she had woken up this morning.

As the trainmaster pulled out of the train station's parking lot to begin the drive home, she sat motionless thinking about the man on the tracks. *Smiling,* she thought. *He was smiling.* She drifted off to a tense sleep.

Claire's car was still up north. She had asked to be dropped off by her condo instead of at the crew base. When the SUV pulled in in front of the condo, the trainmaster offered to have someone bring her car back to her place the next morning. She thanked him and got out.

Walking up the stairs onto the porch, she fumbled in her jacket pocket for her house keys. Once inside, she latched the door and kicked off her boots. She peeled off all her clothes and dumped them into her washing machine, setting it to the sanitary cycle. Then she went straight into the shower to wash the darkness of the day off herself.

CHAPTER 15

In the House

The hot water helped relieve Claire's body aches—climbing up and down ladders, and driving a train, was a lot of physical work for one morning—while the steam, carrying the scent of her lavender body wash, helped calm her nerves.

Half an hour later, in sweat pants and a T-shirt, she paced her entire house, spraying each corner, doorway, and crevice with smokeless sage. She then dosed herself with the protective concoction before cracking open her laptop, looking up anything and everything in the local news referring to pedophile arrests.

As afternoon turned to evening, Claire felt more and more creeped out by the spirit's visit. Why did he make that disgusting comment about Christine?

Claire was standing over the stove, making herself a quick dinner of mac and cheese when the familiar *Jaws* ringtone broke the silence.

"I'm hungry," Claire said to Coal, who was padding around the kitchen. "I'll call her later." Coal expressed no opinion.

She finished cooking and ladled a few large scoops of mac and cheese into a bowl. The cat rubbed against her legs as she sat down at the kitchen table.

"You've got food and water over there, little one," Claire said.

The hot meal and a cup of herbal tea helped her settle down. *Jaws* returned, and she took the call.

"I have been trying to get a hold of you all day. I heard your train hit someone. You okay?" Teri asked, concerned.

"Yeah, I'm fine," Claire replied, heading into the living room. "These things always rattle me a bit," she said.

"Well, yeah," Teri agreed. "The news said he was a pedophile and was about to stand trial?"

"Yeah, it was a pretty bad scene," Claire replied, disgust in her voice. "I still have his image etched in my brain." She closed her eyes tightly, trying to shake it.

"Yeah, but the guy was crap," Teri said, and then they hung up.

Claire heard a loud, slow knock on the wall next to her. One of the ways a spirit communicates is by tapping on walls. It isn't a clear communication, but enough to let you know that they are there.

She ran her fingers through her hair uneasily, knowing that the knocking was sometimes just a jumping-off point, and hoping that it wasn't *him*. But she knew better. It had begun.

She sat quietly on the sofa waiting for another form of communication. After an hour had passed, she believed it was over for the time being. It was just a warning shot, a sign of things to come, no doubt. *He said he wasn't leaving.*

Claire picked up her laptop and started to research spirits that didn't want to cross over. She found that it tended to be because they were afraid of facing the consequences of things they had done in their lives, and were choosing to stay in limbo to avoid having to deal with them in the spirit world. But there was other information that she didn't want to consider. *Dark forces.*

For years after her mother's death, Claire had studied both the Witchcraft and the mediumship sides of her heritage. She had never encountered spirits that didn't want to cross. She knew there were dark forces out there, but she had always strictly followed the rules of the Craft and thereby managed to steer clear of them.

The day's events and the emotional toll they had taken were catching up with her, and she decided to climb into bed and try to sleep.

It didn't happen. She spent the night tossing and turning, the incident playing over and over again like a movie in her mind. When she finally drifted into unconsciousness, chilling words echoing in her ear awakened her. *"She was a sweet little piece of ass when she was younger..."*

Bolting upright and leaping out of bed, she threw on her robe. Startled, Coal ran out of the room. "Stop it. Just stop it!" she yelled into the darkness. "I only speak with spirits that are highly vibrational, and I only do that during the times that I allow them to visit me. I have boundaries. I have times that you can and cannot contact me. And that's it. I am not going to allow you to disturb me any more than you have already. Do you hear me?"

She realized she was shouting. She got her voice under control and continued. "If you want to communicate with me you can try tomorrow. I only allow communications when I am in the kitchen or the living room. Don't ever come to my bedroom again." Claire regained her cool with a deep breath. "I am going back to bed. Good night."

Taking off her robe and getting back under the covers, she replayed the last few minutes in her head. If anyone had heard her telling ghosts to 'only come during visiting hours,' they would have thought she had lost her marbles. But it really worked that way. If they wanted to communicate through her, it had to be on her terms. Otherwise they would be showing up constantly, as they were no longer bound by time as it was understood by mortals.

Suddenly she felt a cold breeze waft by the right side of her head, accompanied by an eerie, low laugh. *"You don't make the rules,"* it sneered, and then it was gone.

The familiar scent of her Mom's perfume instantly calmed her.

Claire remembered trying to tell one of her old boyfriends about the "visits." He kept thinking that the spirits could see her in the bathroom, and when the two of them were being intimate. No matter how many times she explained that it didn't work like that, he'd still get weird every time they had sex, and that really put a damper on the whole love-life thing. Though she found it ironic that, at the end of the day, it was her scar that drove him away, not what was unseen.

As a medium, she found that it wasn't easy having a relationship with someone who wasn't open, and days like the one she'd just had crystalized that fact. She gently caressed the length of her scar with her fingers.

It was just before dawn when she finally drifted off.

* * *

The sun was bright and high in the sky when Claire opened her eyes again. The clock on the small oak nightstand read 12:42 PM. She had only gotten a few hours' sleep, and felt like she had a hangover. She knew it was common to feel this way for a day or two after a traumatic incident. "A normal reaction to an abnormal event," was the phrase the railroad used in their checkup calls.

"Damn," she said softly as she sat up. Putting her robe on, she shuffled off to the kitchen.

After starting the coffee maker, she picked her phone up off the counter. There were twelve missed calls. Four of them were from the EOS counselor—the person on the railroad who deals with employees who are having difficulty for pretty much any reason. Hitting someone on the tracks was certainly one of them. She leaned against the granite countertop and called the counselor back.

"EOS, Bob here," the friendly male voice answered.

"Hi, Bob, Claire Montgomery," she said. "You're calling about the incident yesterday, I'm guessing."

Bob had a nice voice, like he'd missed his calling as a late night jazz DJ. She recounted the facts of the incident, omitting anything supernatural, and then listened as he went through his spiel:

Drink plenty of water, eat well, get some rest, not your fault, and the like.

If sleep was still a problem after tonight, he wanted her to call back, but for now the railroad just wanted her to take three days off and not make any *major life choices.* Kind of an odd concept, she thought. She hung up the phone and then dropped a pod into the coffee maker and pulled her blue ceramic mug from the cabinet.

Sipping the rich liquid, she snuggled into her oversized living room chair and looked through the rest of the messages on her phone. One missed call was from the number 333-333-3333. There was a message, too. She played it, and got nothing but static—the auditory equivalent of the bug fights. She deleted it and continued to listen to her other messages and send reply texts to people who were checking in on her.

The railroad was a tough place, but people also showed up when you needed it most. She was grateful for that.

Lounging around, enjoying the quiet while reading a fast-paced thriller she had picked up at the local bookstore, Claire was almost able to relax. Then her phone rang, disturbing the silence.

Glancing over at it, she saw the number: 333-333-3333. She picked it up and once again all she could hear was static. Hanging up, she went back to her book, but her shoulders were beginning to tense.

A few hours later, as the day was waning, there was a knock on her front door. She sighed and walked over to answer it. It was Teri, bringing paper bags full of Chinese takeout and a warm smile. Claire knew her friend had been worried about her; Teri was nothing if not protective. The funny part was, she always thought she was being slick, but Claire could see through her every time.

"Vegetable Lo Mein and Crab Rangoon for you, and my usual beef and broccoli," Teri said with a casual grin. She walked past Claire to the kitchen, after briefly checking her friend's eyes for any sign of tears.

Grabbing plates from the cabinet, Teri began to babble about being bored and how she was just popping in on the off chance Claire wanted a full Chinese dinner. Rifling through the bag and making more noise than a cat dropped in six inches of water, she turned toward Claire, who was still watching her from the doorway.

"Can you believe they forgot the soy sauce? Who does that?" Teri said, shaking her head in disappointment. "There better be fortune cookies in there, or you're going to have to tell me something I don't already know," she said with a wink.

Teri grabbed her plate and headed into the living room. Claire filled her own plate and joined her friend. They sat on the reclining couches, feet up, with their food and started to make small talk as they ate. About halfway through their dinner,

Teri finally asked the question that had clearly been chewing on her brain. "So, did this guy show up too, after you hit him?"

"Yeah, he did," Claire answered flatly, spinning the lo mein noodles around on her fork. "Where were you today?" she volleyed back, after a moment.

"What do you mean?" Teri asked.

"I smell pot," Claire said, raising her eyebrows.

"Pot? I don't do drugs, you know that," Teri answered defensively.

"I asked where you were," Claire persisted.

"I'm not doing this now." Teri snapped. "You have to stop this shit."

"Just tell me that's not what I smell, Ter."

Teri sat playing with her food for a long moment. "I get a deal on smokes from a guy who's into weed. Cripes, Claire, that was over eight hours ago."

Claire nodded.

"Was he sorry for what he did?" Teri asked, uncharacteristically interested.

"I wouldn't say that," Claire replied pensively.

"Well, what did he say?" Teri pressed, then set her plate on the table. "Look, I know something is going on here, you've been holed up inside since yesterday. You should see your face." She stared at her for a moment, then shrugged and picked her plate back up and plopped her feet up on the coffee table. "I can wait."

Claire took a deep breath and glanced up at the ceiling. Teri's interest was a frustrating thing, because she knew it would be fleeting at best.

"He said, in so many words, that he wasn't going away," Claire said, omitting the shitty comment about Christine. "On top of that, I had Frank on the crew again...you think he flipped out last time? He was saying some really weird shit, I think he might have lost it for good. I wouldn't be surprised if he took early retirement."

"Creepy," Teri said with a scowl.

"I know," Claire went on. "In all my years, I haven't ever had to deal with an earthbound spirit that didn't want to cross over into the light. They usually just go once they see the light or hear their loved ones on the other side call their name. This guy didn't go. I was doing a little reading yesterday, and I guess there are some people who die but they don't want to cross over because they are afraid of what they will face on the other side for the things they have done here. Maybe he's afraid of where he's ultimately going, and maybe he has some kind of delusion that I can change that." Claire set her fork down on the plate and picked up a can of ginger ale.

"Really? So this guy is still here?" Teri asked.

"Yeah," Claire replied stoically.

Just then the lights flickered throughout the house, making the room go from a place of light to a place of darkness, once and then again. Both women looked at each other through the flickering transition, expressionless.

"What the hell was that?" Teri asked as it stopped.

"I think it's him." As quickly as it had darkened, the room became freezing cold, and goose bumps covered the women's arms.

"What's happening?" Teri asked, frightened. They could see their breath. She jumped up as she began to smell a foul odor.

"Do you know what that smell is?" Claire asked emotionlessly, her eyes shining in the darkness.

"It's..." Teri was starting to panic. "It's bad, that's all I know. It's like something burnt, burning..."

"I couldn't label it at first either," Claire said calmly, tracing the scar with her fingers. She sat emotionless, staring at Teri as her friend gathered her belongings and walked toward the door. She knew at that moment that Teri's doubt was definitely being replaced by something else, something Claire never wanted for her...fear.

"I'll call you later, I have to get out of here," Teri said, already halfway out the door.

"I know," Claire said softly, and nodded as Teri glanced at her before shutting the door.

* * *

Shivering as she started the car, Teri looked back at Claire's condo. The chills she felt weren't from the cold; they were from an incredible fear she felt deep within. She was no longer so sure that *this was it*. She was beginning to think that there might be more to life than the part she was used to, but the apprehension she felt with the presence in Claire's house...whatever it was...unnerved her. Shook her. All she knew for sure was that she was in danger somehow. There was no warm and fuzzy feeling, as there had been at the firehouse.

Fishtailing on the snowy road as she sped away, she turned off the radio and drove in silence, processing the possibility that some spirit might be haunting Claire. Teri knew that Claire had always believed that she really connected with the other side, and never doubted it. The only thing she knew for sure was that *something* had been in the house with them, and it sure as shit wasn't Casper.

CHAPTER 16

UNWELCOME GUEST

Teri parked at a haphazard angle in her drive-way and all but sprinted to the front door. Still more than a little spooked, she entered the house and walked through each room, turning on every light in the house. Only then did she take off her coat and boots, which she left lying wet in the middle of the living room.

Still hungry, she opened the refrigerator and found some leftover pizza from a couple of nights ago. She sniffed it to make sure it was still okay before heating it in the microwave. She poured herself a plastic cup of wine and sat down to eat, trying to come to grips with the reality of what she had witnessed in Claire's living room.

She'd felt the temperature go from seventy-some degrees to subzero in a matter of seconds. There was no way that was scientifically possible. She knew it was crazy, but that didn't relieve the knot in her stomach.

Her eyes became heavy as she lay on the green sofa, but she managed to keep them open to watch an episode of *Law and Order: SVU*. The house was quiet for over an hour. Detectives Benson and Stabler caught the bad guy, and Teri sat up, looking around the familiar room.

Nonsense, she said to herself with a chuckle. She walked back through the house, turning off all the lights again as she made her way to the bathroom to wash her face and brush her teeth before snuggling into bed. Within a few minutes, she felt herself drifting off to sleep.

* * *

The ring of the house phone jolted Teri awake. Glancing at the clock, she saw it read 3:33 AM. *Who the hell is calling me at this hour? This can't be good,* she thought.

"Hello," Teri said. "Hello, who is calling?" she asked again after a moment.

There was loud static on the line. She pulled the phone away from her ear and looked at the caller ID: 333-333-3333. *That's strange,* she thought. She hung up and rolled onto her stomach to try to fall back to sleep. After a few changes of position, she once again felt herself drifting off.

Just a few hours later came the annoying "Beep! Beep! Beep!" of Teri's alarm, which had been set for 6:21 AM. For some reason, setting it for a random time rather than the turn of an hour or half-hour, woke her up faster. Fishing for her phone, she hit the snooze button and closed her eyes again, but she was already awake.

Lying on top of her blue and gray Dallas Cowboys comforter, she stared up at the ceiling, reflecting on the day before and the strangeness of it all. Remembering the call in the middle of the night, she furrowed her brow and grabbed her house phone from the mostly stable stack of books and magazines she used as a makeshift end table. She looked at the caller ID and saw that she had remembered the details correctly. The number was 333-333-3333, and the time had been 3:33. The chill she'd felt the night before was returning. She called Claire.

"Good morning," her friend said calmly on the other end of the line.

"Umm, I got a phone call last night at 3:33 AM and it was from 333-333-3333. What does that mean?" Teri asked uneasily.

"I think," Claire began in a matter-of-fact voice, "that you should just enjoy your day off and make plans for us to have dinner at your house tonight. I will bring something from Donorfrio's. Don't worry too much about the phone call…it's just a phone call," she said reassuringly.

Great, Claire said to herself as she hung up the phone. She immediately went to the tall wooden bookcase and took out a few books she used for research when she was stumped by some aspect of the spirit world. She knew that this guy was angry, based on the energy she felt and the heaviness that accompanied him. But there was something else: the smell. *She knew that smell.*

She scratched the scar on her face. She could feel the energy; it was menacing. She hadn't felt it since that night so many years ago. Yesterday it had been almost tangible. It was so heavy it had apparently been able to latch onto Teri, and she knew that was a situation that could become dangerous very fast.

Spirits possess different levels of ability, and if they are able to come into physical contact with you, you have a problem. She knew that scenario well. It's not like you can call the electric company and put in a work order to get rid of it.

Having spoken to the counselor yesterday after the incident, she knew that she was on a company-mandated, three-day, self-care hiatus. That gave her plenty of time to figure out a way to cross this guy over.

Scouring her books and researching online, she decided that she would try to keep him civil by answering any questions he might have. *At the very least,* she thought, *that should keep him out of Teri's hair.*

She retrieved a three-legged table from her garage and carried it inside, letting it warm up and adjust to the indoor temperature. The art of table tipping dates back to the 1800s, when it was discovered that a table could be used as a means of communication with the spirit world. Via the table's movement, one could receive answers to yes-or-no questions.

She remembered being amazed the first time she did some table tipping with her mother. It was beyond explanation how a table could lift itself up and tip over without anyone touching it.

She thought that this would be the best as well as the safest way to get answers. Plus, a spirit board or Ouija board would freak Teri out. A plain table would be a much more acceptable option. Teri wouldn't be scared, and the spirits would still be able to answer questions—if she could get her to open up to the idea.

Satisfied with the plan, she realized that most of this was better off done in private, but she felt that it would be good for Teri to see the preparation that was required to keep the two of them safe, as well as asking the spirit world for help.

Calling Donofrio's to place an order for chicken Marsala and steak dinners, both of which she knew Teri loved, she set the phone down and walked outside. Her car was there. The railroad had left it unlocked with the keys in the ignition. She was grateful that she didn't have to go all the way back to Alderon to get it herself. She started the car, turned the heat on high, and then returned to the house to grab the table.

Placing it on the back seat, she locked up the house and headed to the restaurant. She was lucky and found a parking space not far from the entrance. She placed the food on the floor on the passenger side so the heat would keep it warm on the ride to Teri's.

When she pulled up, Teri already had the front door open, waiting for her. "I got us chicken Marsala and steak; we can split it," Claire said with a warm smile.

"You had me thinking about this craziness all day," Teri grumbled.

"I told you that I would be over, and you need to just trust me from here forward," Claire said calmly, handing over the food. "I have to grab one more thing; I'll be right back," she added as she returned to the car.

She struggled to open Teri's front door with the table in her arms, but managed to get inside without damaging it or the door frame.

"What is that for?" Teri called out from the kitchen. "I have enough crap in this place already," she griped, walking back into the living room clutching the dinnerware.

"It's for later," Claire replied nonchalantly.

"For what?" Teri asked again. "And do you want white or red?"

"Neither of us is going to have wine tonight," Claire said, looking straight into her friend's eyes. "Tonight you are going to help me cross the guy from yesterday over, and you need to keep your vibration high. No wine." She glared at her to emphasize the point.

"I don't know what you think I am going to do here, but my only plans are to watch. I want no part of this," Teri said flatly, fear coming through every word she spoke.

"Teri, the call you got last night was from *him*. You are already a part of this. And you *are* going to help with this, or you *are* going to be dealing with him more often than you think," Claire warned. "Look," she said, trying to soften her tone, "fear, like the fear you had last night, is a form of energy—and spirits thrive on energy. You have to control your emotions with this...*especially* fear."

Teri sat quietly as the words sank in. She knew what she'd felt in the room with them last night; she also knew that the feeling had not gone away. She'd felt it instantly again, the second she'd walked in the house after returning from shopping that afternoon. It wasn't something that could be described in words. It was just something she felt and knew.

Claire made herself busy while Teri continued to sit quietly, processing everything she had said. She opened the bag of food and filled both plates with a little of everything.

"Do you have steak sauce?" Claire asked.

As if a spell had been broken, Teri was back in the present and looked down at the plate that Claire had prepared for her.

"It should be in the refrigerator door, near the chocolate syrup, if I have any," Teri answered and stood up from the couch. "I'll be right back."

If this is how Claire feels all the time, Teri thought, *I want no part of it.* She stealthily grabbed a bottle of Merlot from under the counter and took a long drink, then returned it. She grabbed the steak sauce from the refrigerator as Claire shook her head knowingly and took a bite of chicken.

Teri handed her the steak sauce and, after dragging a fry through the ketchup, began to cut up her steak.

"Think you have enough ketchup?" Claire asked as she looked at the huge blob on Teri's plate.

"Nope, definitely gonna need more before this meal's over," Teri said sarcastically. "So what do you mean I need to help you?" she asked between bites.

Claire chewed slowly and deliberately, buying herself time to formulate the words she was going to use to get Teri on board.

"Well, he—the spirit—obviously is here, and he is being a bit of a menace. He called my phone several more times today, too. I didn't put it all to-gether until you called me this morning," Claire said.

Teri sat still, listening.

Finishing up the last of her chicken Marsala, Claire again began to put things into words that Teri would understand, and hopefully be less likely to freak out about.

"I think he is afraid to cross over," Claire said.

Teri looked at her blankly.

"We are going to use the table as a medium between us and him, to help us ask him some yes and no questions...and then we are going to cut an opening into the next realm...call in his loved ones...and send him packing," Claire explained.

"Yeah, Claire, you'll inform me when the shuttle lands," Teri quipped. "So, to be clear, we're going to ask a dead guy questions, using a table. Then, we're going to cut an opening in space and send him on his way. You are one hundred percent nuts," she finished flatly.

"No, we really are going to do all that, and I need you for the table part or else I would just do it myself. It will be okay; I promise," Claire said with as much conviction as she could muster.

"No is right. Not happening. I don't want to do anything with the table thing, and I certainly don't want to do anything with some weirdo spirit," Teri said, waving her arms dismissively.

"You really don't have an option," Claire replied with a shrug. "He is here and he can visit you, Teri," she continued, leaning closer and looking deeper into her eyes. "And I mean any-time he wants, and any place he wants."

"Well, can't you just spray that weird ghost killer shit you're always spraying around and tell him to go away?" Teri asked.

"Nope, it doesn't work that way. I think that if we just ask him a couple of questions he will be willing to meet up with his family on the other side," Claire said, rubbing her forehead pensively. "I hope."

"So what is this table tipping thing?" Teri asked, and Claire knew that the wall was at least cracking, if not falling. She explained how they were going to stage the entire room, the table, and each other to help keep them protected from the menacing energy this guy was giving off.

They would sit on opposite sides of the table and call in their spirit guides, asking the spirit realm to help them with answers. Knowing that this information was bringing Teri to the brink of overload, she waited a few minutes before telling her that the table might lift up off the floor and not to be nervous.

"Lift off the floor! You are killing me. I always liked you but thought you were a freak, and now here you are telling me a table is going to lift off the floor to give you answers—I don't think so!" Teri stood up angrily. For the second night in a row, she wasn't going to finish dinner.

"Take your table and all that crap and go home. I can't deal with this," Teri said, her voice iron with resolve.

Standing up, Claire brought her plate to the kitchen and scraped it clean before putting it in the sink. She put on her coat and stepped into her little black boots. Picking up the table and walking to the door, she turned to face Teri.

"You'll be calling me soon enough," she said, turning and navigating her way out the door.

The sudden smell of burnt hair and sulfur in the hot sun made her gag.

Pulling out of the driveway, Claire turned to look at the house as she shifted her car into first gear. Through the window, she could make out a gray mist of ectoplasm hovering near Teri.

CHAPTER 17

THE DETECTIVE

As she pulled into her driveway, Claire spotted an unfamiliar car parked directly across from her house. She knew it was occupied by the exhaust billowing from its tailpipe into the frigid night air, and she knew it was an official vehicle of some kind because who the hell else drove a four-door Chevy Caprice?

Looking in her review mirror as she parked, she saw a large male figure climbing out of the sedan.

What is he *doing here?* she thought, agitated. As though it wasn't bad enough having Teri flip out on her, now she had this jerk Bellissimo hunting her down.

Probably wants to make fun of me too, she thought, shaking her head in disgust.

"Claire," Bellissimo called in a booming voice as she opened her car door.

She turned to face him, but stood in silence, not wanting to speak before she had her emotions under control. But he seemed to be waiting her out, too. "Hello, Detective, what brings you here?" she finally asked. "You didn't seem too interested in what I had to say a week ago."

"I've come to ask you a few more questions," Bellissimo said, taking a few steps closer and bridging the distance between them. He was now close enough that Claire could see his breath steaming.

"I told you everything I know, Detective. I really don't want to deal with this anymore. I've had a couple of bad days and tonight was no picnic either. I don't want to waste my time trying to explain things to someone that obviously doesn't believe me."

"What I want to know is: Did you know the latest train victim?" Bellissimo asked.

"What the hell are you talking about?" Claire asked, bewildered.

"How is it that you just happened to be on the train that took the life of Wayne Douglas Daniels?" Bellissimo fired back.

"I planned that trip last week, it was pre-scheduled on my work calendar. You can look to see when I wrote it in, or check with the railroad," Claire replied. "Also, Detective," she added sarcastically, "if you can explain how a train, which travels a prescribed route on stationary tracks, can hunt a person down, you're a hell of a lot smarter than I am."

"I don't know what your game is, lady," Bellissimo said, jabbing a finger at her. "I don't know what you think you are going to get out of this, saying that you, for lack of a better description, speak to dead people. But I intend to find out. If you or your friend are involved in any way, you are both going to see how the criminal justice system really works." Bellissimo had moved close enough now that Claire could feel his breath on her cheek.

Cigar or Cloves?

"What the hell are you talking about?" she asked, exasperated.

"What am I talking about? You were on the train that ran over a pedophile who was involved in a sex-slave ring. When they searched his house they found a holding room and pictures of his slaves, and Christine was one of them. So why is it that you told me that I should look for a guy named Doug, and now that very guy, who you told us to look for, gets run over by a train with you in the cab, leaving us no way to question him?"

The front porch lights from some of the surrounding houses had now come on, and Claire could see a few of her neighbors peeking out of their windows. "I've had enough for one day," she said, and turned her back on the detective. With shaking hands, she put her key into the lock and opened her front door.

She was aware that Bellissimo was walking away behind her, but without looking back, she entered her home, locked the door, and turned off the outside light.

Safely inside the condo, her body began to tremble. She wasn't sure what was upsetting her the most: that Teri still thought she was a freak, or that Bellissimo believed that she was somehow involved with this horrific sex-slave ring. Either way, she had no one to talk to about it.

CHAPTER 18

CONTACT

Claire could hear the rumble of the Caprice's motor and the crunch of ice as the detective drove away. She slumped to the floor of the entry hall. The events of the last week, and now this new information, were just too much.

Alone, Claire lay on the floor for a long time, softly crying with frustration and fear. The wide range of emotions she felt seemed to punch her in the chest with each sob. Teri was pissed at her. Bellissimo thought she was a murderer, or a vigilante, or both. And she still hadn't had time to process her feelings about the first accident, never mind the second.

She understood Teri's anger. Her friend was scared that what Claire had been telling her for so many years was true, and she couldn't accept it. But the more frightened Teri became, the lower her vibration went, and the easier it would be for the spirit to attach to her and use that negative energy to continue his mischief...or worse.

Bellissimo's beliefs, though, couldn't be justified. There was no reason to think she was involved—she'd come to him! Doug had committed suicide out of desperation; the fact that Claire had been on that train would have been purely coincidental—if she believed in coincidence. What Bellissimo couldn't know, of course, was that Doug was still fighting his demons even after death. His spirit was not going to go away quietly—she was sure of it.

The wheels in Claire's mind kept spinning. Who could she turn to? Who would understand? She wasn't sure how she could make things right, and she also wasn't sure how she was going to protect Teri. She just knew that at this moment she was too overwhelmed to see a way out.

Shivering from the cold floor, she opened her eyes and looked out the window. The sky was starting to turn a dull yellow in the distance. She forced herself upright and felt her muscles aching from the stress and emotions that seemed to have settled into her back and shoulders.

Opening her mouth to call for Coal, who had been cautiously watching her, she felt a tightness in her jaw and realized that the pain in her head had turned from a dull ache to a full-blown throb. Giving the cat a few quick strokes down her back, Claire walked toward the bathroom, feeling eighty-five years old.

Opening the shower curtain, she turned the water on. The smell of the steam, mixed with the fragrance of her soap, filled the room.

She undressed and stood looking into the mirror, silently watching herself disappear from view. *If only it were that easy for all of this to disappear,* she thought as she stepped into the shower.

Fifteen minutes later, she was feeling more relaxed. Her muscles weren't as tight, and the throb in her head wasn't as strong as it had been. She felt more confident, and ready to put the pity party she had been having behind her.

"Pull yourself together," she said into the mirror. "Teri needs you, and you aren't going to be of any use to her if you are a wallowing mess. You are going to wipe that smug look off that fucking Bellissimo's face, too."

Still looking at her reflection, she saw her eyes change color, as they often did when she felt the "others" close by. They became a deeper shade of green. Knowing that they were watching and waiting for her to get her head out of her ass, she was enveloped by calm. She wasn't sure how things would work out, but she knew that she wasn't alone any longer and that her spirit guides and family were close by and ready to help.

"Trust." The word echoed through her mind like a warm breeze on an early fall day.

Walking to her bedroom, she gently pulled down the covers so as not to disturb Coal, who was sprawled out on the end of the bed. She slid between the sheets, intending to get a few hours of sleep before she headed back to work.

No wonder Tony had been so abrasive, she thought, beginning to see his perspective. *It really does look like I know a lot more than I do.*

The thought also elevated the concern she had for her friend. This was uncharted territory for her, for the most part. She had not had to deal with the darker side of the spirit world since she was a child and, based on what she'd felt and the sickening color of that ectoplasm hovering near Teri, she was certain that she would need all of her wits about her.

* * *

Seven hours later, Claire reached over Coal's purring body and turned off the alarm before it rang. She stumbled out of bed and into the kitchen to make coffee. She needed to get that first jolt of caffeine into her before she tried to untangle her situation.

Taking the cup into the living room, she was just about to sit down when the *Jaws* theme pierced the morning quiet. With a swipe of her finger she answered the call. Before she could utter a word, Teri was already frantically blurting things Claire couldn't make out, her voice a high-pitched shriek.

"Slow down," Claire said calmly.

"I can't slow down!" Teri shouted into the phone. "What did you bring here last night? You need to get over here *now!*" she screamed.

"Okay, I will be there in about half an hour, let me get dressed and take a shower. It will help you out to relax a bit until I get there," Claire offered.

"Take a shower? This...this, whatever it is has to stop! Just get your ass over here!" Teri snarled accusingly.

"I'm coming," Claire said as she hung up and began rummaging through her drawers, looking for a pair of jeans.

Just about half an hour later, Claire was about to knock on Teri's door when Teri appeared and swung it open.

"What's going on? You look like shit!" Claire asked as she entered the house. Once inside, she could immediately feel the thickness of the air and the sense of dread emanating from her friend. She stopped in her tracks and began to sniff the air. *Burning hair and sulfur.*

"You tell *me* what's going on! You brought that damn table and now things in my house are completely fucked. The clocks are going crazy, the lights are turning on and off, the fan in the bedroom won't turn off, and someone keeps pounding on my ceiling!"

"I tried to—" Claire was cut off mid-sentence.

"You tried to what? Make me a fruit loop with all this crap?" Teri said with so much force she almost knocked Claire over.

"No. I tried to tell you that there is some really dark energy here and it wants you," Claire replied sternly, not stepping back.

"What do you mean dark energy, and what do you mean it *wants me*? This is part of your voodoo bullshit and I don't want any part of it. I've warned you about that a thousand times, Claire!"

"You know that guy I hit the other day?" Claire began calmly. "Well, he is the guy that kidnapped Christine. Detective Bellissimo was waiting at my house when I came home last night and he accused me of knowing more than I did."

"What does that have to do with me?" Teri asked, nearly exploding with anger.

"A lot. I think that the reason you are having so many things happen is because Doug is trying to get to me through you," Claire said, trying to remain calm.

"A ghost? You're something else. You go out there and play with your invisible friends, and now you tell me you brought one back for me that's making my life a living hell for no apparent reason. Get out of here and take your friends with you," Teri concluded, throwing her hands in the air.

"Let me explain," Claire said, trying to keep her composure.

"No! I said get out!" Teri marched to the door and swung it open. Claire shook her head and walked out into the cold.

Once outside the house, the air no longer felt so heavy, like it wanted to choke her. *What am I going to do?* Claire asked herself as she walked to her car. "Mom, what do I do?" she called out to the wind.

A few minutes later, she pulled up outside of the Bottom of the Mug coffee shop. She'd grab a cup of coffee and maybe some breakfast while she waited for Moonshadows: Gifts for the Spirit to open in just under an hour.

Thea, the owner, was a wise woman whose shop offered a variety of metaphysical wares for serious practitioners and curious amateurs alike. Claire was hoping that maybe there was a book or something—anything—that could help her make sense of all that was going on.

When her bacon and eggs arrived, Claire picked at them, checking her watch every few minutes and waiting as the hands on the old-fashioned dial crawled painfully slowly toward ten AM. Finally, it was close enough to start the three-block walk.

Mmmm. Warm gingerbread.

"Hello, Thea," Claire called, exactly one minute after ten. The string of bells on the door chimed lightly as she entered the quaint shop.

"Well hello, Claire. Haven't seen you in a while," Thea said, more like an accusation than a greeting.

"I have been super busy with work, and just haven't had a lot of time to delve into fun stuff," Claire replied. "I am looking for books on tough mediumship cases, maybe something a little on the dark side. Do you have anything like that?" She tried not to show her anxiety.

"Hmmm, I am not sure if I have anything like that. Let me look in the back, we just got some old books in that I haven't really looked at too closely yet," Thea said, and disappeared behind the curtains she used to separate the back room from the main floor of the shop.

When she reappeared, she said, "I had a few back there that looked interesting and may be what you are looking for. Some were privately owned—I got them from an estate sale in Middlebury."

Thea handed Claire a pile of books. Some were new; others had torn dust jackets, while still others had a thin layer of dust on them from sitting around for so long. Picking up the first book, Claire opened it to the middle. The smell of mildew rushed into her nostrils.

She set it down on top of a separate pile of books she was certain she didn't want. Picking up the next one, she opened the front cover. It had obviously been written by someone intending to show their superior knowledge of the subject, yet offered no real substance and had nothing to teach her. She continued to peruse the stack. Several others were just not what she was looking for. Some had religious warnings about the occult being the devil's work, and others just made it sound like a taboo subject that could only be discussed in a dark room where no one could hear you.

The very last book in the pile was intriguing. Before picking it up she could already smell burnt hair and sulfur permeating the entire volume. She knew that whoever had owned this book had been affiliated with the dark side. Before she could turn it over, she was struck by an intense image of red lights in her mind's eye. Flipping the hefty volume, she saw that the deep-red leather cover was graced with images representing the eight pagan holidays, surrounded by a circle of thirteen candles representing the thirteen full moons of the year. The words DWELL BEYOND IF THOU DELVE BEYOND HERE were printed in threatening, bold black type.

Claire shuddered. She knew the author had chosen the title and imagery to ward off anyone who might be just dabbling.

Skimming the book, Claire read a few sentences that seemed to jump out at her. This book would be of help.

"Thanks, Mom," Claire mouthed, gazing up at the ceiling. Then, trying to sound bored, she told Thea, "This one looks interesting. I'll take it."

After paying for the book, she headed for the door and was just about to leave the small shop when she heard Thea call after her, "The dark doesn't provide light."

CHAPTER 19

No Rest for the Weary

Claire could hear Thea's words echoing in her mind as she walked into her condo. She headed straight for the couch and plopped down with the large, antiquated book. Despite the warning, she knew the only way she would be able to help Teri was by looking into the dark side. This was something that she had avoided since that night so long ago. Her stomach coiled and flip-flopped.

"Mom, I know you pointed me to this, but I am not sure what you want me to do," Claire said aloud, rubbing her fingers over the book's cover.

As she flipped it open, a foreboding chill ran up her spine. She knew it was a warning not to enter this realm, but she had no choice.

A black clown's head with ram's horns sprouting from its skull, no mouth, and pale-gray eyes with no pupils stared back at her. There was nothing else on the page; no doubt it was a final warning to go no further.

Turning past the menacing image, she started at the beginning. She read about ways in which earthbound spirits could play tricks and attach themselves to humans. It seemed like a manual of sorts for bad human beings who wanted to commit suicide and then terrorize living people from beyond the grave.

The more she read, the more she could feel the coldness her mother had taught her to block out as a child after that terrible night.

"Mommy, it's burnt toast. It's burnt toast," Claire had insisted.

"Claire," her mother had said sternly, "it's not burnt toast. Tell him he doesn't exist to you." The memory was faded in parts, but she remembered the beginning of the evening clearly. She had been shaken awake by giant, cold, claw-like hands. They lifted her straight up into the air, off her small mattress by her face and neck, sneering, "Help no one, no one!"

She'd tried to scream through her tears over and over again: "You don't exist!" But the claws were digging into her throat and no sound would come out.

Her mother heard the thrashing around and came running into the room. She jumped onto the entity, yelling something in a different, almost guttural language and then waved her arm forcefully toward the window. There had been a cracking sound, almost like dull thunder, and then the window burst, sending shards of glass everywhere.

The entity was forced through the window at an incredible speed, sending her mother crashing headlong into the wall. His claws scratched deeply into the left side of little Claire's face as he was jerked away from her, cutting through her flesh as though it were a stick of butter.

In the silence that followed, her mom sat still and expressionless on the floor, looking over at Claire as the little girl shivered in fear across the room. Her mother began to clutch her chest, trying to gain control of her breathing. Claire sat in shock as blood poured from her wound.

"If you don't want this in your life, Claire," she said in a strained but comforting voice, tossing a towel toward little Claire, "then you can never let it in."

Her mom paused and began to cough and gurgle. Blood trickled from the corner of her mouth. "That means you don't acknowledge it in any form. You don't read about it, you don't look at it, you leave it alone."

Her mom's body began to shake and Claire screamed, crawling to her side.

"Mommy, no! Mommy, don't go!"

Her mother opened her eyes slowly for the final time, and grabbed Claire by the hair.

"Don't you ever forget that smell, Claire. Don't you ever forget that smell."

End of her mother's life. End of memory.

Claire read on. About incredibly evil people who could continue to carry on with their unsavory ways even after death by choosing to not cross over, and by following the dark forces' instructions—like these.

They preyed upon the scared and the weak, and unfortunately, getting rid of such a dark spirit wasn't easy. Evil didn't have particular parameters to constrain it, or rules it played by. Claire was uncertain where her safe place would be when confronting this entity, or whether the sacred circle of protection she had always relied on could hold back this evil. It wasn't long before questions began to pile up. *Demon? Yeah right*, she murmured uneasily, and drifted off into a late morning nap.

* * *

The ringing of her work phone jolted Claire upright and she fumbled around the coffee table to find it. Glancing at the caller ID, she saw it was one of the engineers she supervised.

"Good afternoon. Claire Montgomery," she said.

"This is Rick," a man's more-than-annoyed voice came from the other end. "I need some forms to get my new prescription safety glasses. I told you a couple of weeks ago and I am still waiting. I'm not going to wait much longer. Do you have them or what?" He spoke in a voice that sounded a lot like Eeyore from *Winnie the Pooh*.

"I am going to be in the area in a little while," she said, looking at the clock. It was noon. "I'll bring them with me."

She rubbed her forehead. The dull headache she had been experiencing for several days was still there. The click at the other end of the line, without so much as a goodbye, let her know that Rick might sound harmless like Eeyore, but he was just as passive-aggressive as the rest of the guys.

"Nice talking to you, too." Claire said. She looked at the phone's background image, a photo of herself and Teri at Sterling Pond. They had hiked up there one day last fall when the colors were at their peak. She sat still, staring wistfully at it. The rich oranges and reds popped out against the yellows and greens to compose a spectacular view. Closing her eyes, she could almost hear the crinkling sound of the leaves.

The night before had been rough. She was tired and felt as though she had a major hangover from the confusion. Looking over at her work boots, she rolled her eyes. A quick mental calculation let her know that a one-hour nap wasn't going to get it done, and that it was going to be one of those days.

"No rest for the weary," she said, easing her legs over the edge of the couch. After mapping out the rest of her day, she printed out the sheets that Rick needed and packed her work bag.

If she left now, she would have enough time to stop in at Moonshadows again before it closed. She knew from the thoughts and flickering images that had popped into her mind before she had fallen asleep that she needed to return.

* * *

She met up with a few Federal Railroad Administration agents when she was leaving the crew base and ended the conversation as quickly as she could manage. Still, having learned long ago how to separate work from everything else that was going on, she was thankful she'd run into them. Those few moments that she'd spent talking about work and getting information from the agents had helped her state of mind.

As the two agents were getting back into their vehicle, she had an epiphany. *This is how it works. Once I let my guides and Mom and Nana help, things fall into place. Why do I doubt*, she scolded herself.

Checking the time, she saw that it was only three in the afternoon and Thea would definitely still be open. She backed her car out of the parking lot and headed toward town.

Using a little trick she'd learned as a teenager honing her skills, she projected a nice parking place. Envisioning it in her mind, as she approached the shop she saw the white lights of a van backing out of the very space she had envisioned.

Flinging the car door open, she headed inside.

Gingerbread.

"Well, hello, Claire. Twice in one day, huh," Thea said with an amused look.

"I am wondering if you can help me with something else, Thea," Claire asked in a voice that seemed to come from deep within her. "I need to know if you know any women that practice Witchcraft?"

"Yes, I do," Thea replied without hesitation.

"Do you think any of them would be willing to speak with me?" Claire asked.

Thea let out a laugh. "They are very secretive. Though I dabble in a little of this and a little of that, I generally work alone. But the ladies you are looking for were also born into the Craft."

"I suspected that you practiced, with some of the items you purchase. My gut told me you were a witch, but I respected your privacy. Not too many people come in here looking for smokeless sage. The wannabes are always looking to flaunt it and draw attention to themselves, like being a witch is a fashion statement. The true are always guarded and careful when letting others know," Thea said casually.

"Thank you. I have felt so alone since leaving Salem, Massachusetts to come up here for work. This town is pretty small, and folks just don't seem to understand. I have never wanted to call attention to myself. In Salem it is acceptable to practice and to be exactly who I am, authentically and with no excuses. Here, with no Coven, it has been a challenge," Claire admitted.

Tears were starting to form in her eyes as Thea gave her names and Claire began to input them into the contact list on her cell. The calmness and serenity of knowing she was no longer alone was overwhelming.

CHAPTER 20

BRINGING IN THE GUNS

Claire sat on her couch staring at her phone for several minutes before finally picking it up from the table. She scrolled through her contacts, landing on a name she hadn't thought about for a long time. *Lola Davies.* Her finger hovered above the screen; she wasn't sure if she should text or call. She sat a little longer, pondering her options. There weren't any.

She tapped the call button with a fast jab of her finger, like she thought it would hurt and wanted to get it over with. Almost as quickly, she heard Lola's voice on the other end, picking up after a single ring. She could tell from her tone that the other woman wasn't sure who was calling. Claire thought about hanging up for a second, but didn't.

"Hello Lola, this is Claire, Claire Montgomery. We met a few years ago at the fire and fertility celebration for Beltane in Swanton. I am wondering if you have a few minutes to chat?"

"Oh, hello, Claire. Of course I remember you. It has been a long time. I am on my way out to the barn to feed the animals dinner, but can give you a call back in a few minutes if that's okay?"

"Sure, that will be fine. I really need some advice and I look forward to your call," Claire replied.

"Great, talk to you in a few," Lola said, and was gone, probably already headed to the barn. Claire liked that quality about her; it had captured her attention during the Beltane celebration weekend. Lola was straightforward, and she did exactly what she said she was going to do.

Although Lola Davies was slight in stature, her presence and aura filled the space around her with pure energy. Claire had been immediately drawn to her because of that. Lola had long, dark hair that had a way of bouncing back into place perfectly with every turn of her head. Her tanned and muscular arms were covered in tattoos. Although each was a separate work of art, collectively the tattoos told the ongoing story of Lola's life. Each arm was like a tale from two completely different times that melded together between her upper chest and collarbone area, which was adorned with the faces of each of her children, all surrounded by flowers. A tattoo of the sun sat on one shoulder blade and one of the moon on the other. Just under the row of faces was a ribbon with the words EVERY DAY IS FILLED WITH LOVE cascading across it.

Claire had no tattoos. She wasn't sure if it was because she didn't want to undergo the pain it must entail, because of the amount of time she would have to spend sitting still, or because she didn't think there was anything she would ever want stenciled on her forever. But that didn't stop her from admiring the story Lola was brave enough to share through the lovely artwork adorning the canvas of her body.

Claire dragged her thoughts back to the task at hand, and continued to scroll through her phone's contact list. Calling a second number, she waited for a ringtone but instead got voice mail. She left a short message, asking for a call back, emphasizing the urgency of her need.

Gia Garviano was a vivacious and over-the-top bubbly woman, but she had a strong business sense and a way of putting things into words that let you know that she was always on top of her game. Her big brown eyes and olive skin framed by thick, black hair made her look like anything but the girl next door. She oozed a certain type of sex appeal mixed with mystery that was hard to put into words.

Gia had a presence that could only be described as luminous. When Claire had first met her, Gia's inner light had shone like a beacon, letting her know that the woman was a kindred spirit. Witches and those who were truly spiritual always recognized each other by their energetic fingerprints.

Claire acknowledged that she was very much a solitary witch and medium; she had kept her spiritual side to herself almost all her life. Since moving to St. Albans, her isolation had become even more extreme. She had attended many rituals, but always watched from the outer circle. She felt truly alone. And now, reaching out to others for help and guidance was making the hair on the back of her neck stand up. She wasn't sure what to expect, but she knew that controlling whoever or *what*ever was feeding off Teri required more expertise than she possessed. She needed backup.

CHAPTER 21

PURSUIT

Her face, back and chest covered in sweat, Teri leaned heavily into her basement door. To the blare of the TV and stereo, cranked up as loud as they could go, she added the pounding of nails. Panting, she finally hammered the last two-by-four across the door.

"Leave me alone!" she screamed, her ragged voice barely audible above the History Channel's latest Hitler special, competing with Bruce Springsteen's "Born to Run." Suddenly she heard a thunderous crack and spun around, breathing heavily, the hammer still clenched in her hand.

Two police officers slowly approached her, arms open as if to say, "It's okay, whack job, we're not here to hurt you."

"You broke my door down?" Teri asked, disoriented.

"We pounded on it and yelled at you that we were going to break it down unless you opened it for us," the younger of the two cops said, as he edged closer to her.

Teri looked down at the hammer in her hands and slowly bent over and set it on the floor. The older cop turned off the stereo and TV a moment later, and they both stood looking at Teri, giving her a comfortable five feet of personal space.

"What seems to be the problem, ma'am?" the first officer asked, concerned. "We got a call from your neighbors. They were worried about you. Everything all right here?"

"She's turned me into a nut!" Teri blurted, shaking her head. "They won't stop playing with my head, they won't stop! Please, make it stop," she pleaded with the officer, sitting down on the floor and rocking back and forth with her face in her hands.

A third man walked slowly into the room. He stepped between the two officers, looked down at Teri crumpled on the floor, and motioned for them to go outside. He dropped to one knee beside her.

"Hey there," he said warmly. "Don't I know you from somewhere?"

She recognized his voice, and glanced up. *Detective Asshole Bellissimo,* she said to herself.

"Yeah, you're the donut guy," she grumbled.

"Well that's a good sign," he said sarcastically. "Your sense of humor is still intact."

She wouldn't look him in the eye, and the smile left his face. "Do you want to talk about it?" he asked softly.

"Yes," she said defensively, finally looking up at him. "But I know you aren't going to listen, so what's the point?"

He stared down at her thoughtfully, his large, dark eyes evaluating her.

"Well, I can get the officers to leave if you can make me feel good about what we're doing here," he offered.

"I know it looks bad," Teri said, "and I don't know why they stopped just because you are here. I know how it looks. I know!"

"C'mon," Bellissimo said, offering his hand and helping Teri to her feet. "Let's talk in your living room, where it's more comfortable, okay?"

Teri nodded reluctantly and they sat side by side on the green sofa, still piled high with clean laundry.

"I don't know how to explain this," Teri said softly, frustration in her voice.

The detective nodded reassuringly. "It's all right. How about starting with something simple, like why you had both the stereo and TV blaring?"

Teri sighed, exhausted. "They have been banging on the walls and ceiling for two days. I can't sleep," she said, her voice cracking. "I just couldn't take it anymore, and when they started pounding on the tables in my basement, I just...I lost it," she said, breaking down in tears.

He reached out and grabbed her hand in his firmly. "It's okay, just relax," he said, comforting her. "Now, 'they'...*who* is banging on the walls?"

Teri sat up and looked directly into his eyes. "It's a ghost."

Bellissimo clenched his jaw and blinked slowly three times, holding her gaze. "A ghost," he repeated, staring at her.

Teri exploded as she stood up from the couch. "Do you think I really wanted to go with her to tell you about fucking talking dead people? Do you? I'm not crazy! There's something here!"

"Just relax," Bellissimo said, trying to calm her.

"Relax? *Relax*? You fuckin' relax, Detective! You aren't the one with a haunted house! I don't even believe in this shit!" She sat back down, wrapping her arms around herself and rocking back and forth.

Bellissimo rose to his feet and began pacing. "Are you tired?" he asked softly.

"Exhausted," she finally answered in a scratchy voice.

"Anything going on with family or friends that might be kinda stressful lately?" He was trying to keep his voice casual, not wanting to trigger another outburst.

"No," she began, and then stopped. "Well, my best friend has a problem...and it's bothering me now too, I guess."

He nodded. "You think a good night's sleep might help put your mind to rest about what's going on with Claire?"

"I don't know. Maybe," she murmured. "I'm really tired. I've been up for two days."

He put his hands on her shoulders and nudged her backward into the sofa. He smiled at her.

"Would you like me to get you a glass of milk?" he asked, searching her eyes.

"No," Teri replied, unnerved by his attention. "I don't want to keep you."

"Wait here," he said with a nod and walked into Teri's cluttered kitchen. "Where do you keep the glasses?" he called out, as she sat motionless on the couch.

"Cabinet next to the sink," she replied through a jaw-cracking yawn.

As the detective rummaged around her kitchen, Teri scanned the living room walls and ceiling with suspicion and fear.

Bellissimo looked out at her. "Do you want something to eat?" he asked.

"No," she said, shaking her head. She was tired, frightened, and emotionally raw, but she had absolutely no appetite.

He returned to the living room, a glass of milk in his hand. "Here you go," he said, handing her the cup and two small pills he pulled from his jacket pocket.

"What are these?" Teri asked, taking them from his hand.

"The answer to your prayers, I think," he replied.

Teri popped the pills and took a sip of milk. "I know this is a bad time to ask but, you're not a murderer or anything, are you? Not gonna roofie me?" she asked.

"Nah," he replied, grinning. "Too messy."

"Please don't leave," Teri whispered. "I promise I'm not crazy."

He sat down on the chair next to the couch. "I got you," he said softly. "Go to sleep."

Teri closed her eyes as Bellissimo sat watching her.

"They just keep messing with my head. They keep messing with my head..." she murmured and finally drifted off.

Claire talks to dead people, and this girl is all over the place, Bellissimo thought as he stood up and walked toward the broken door.

Trying to be as quiet as possible, he rummaged around in the toolkit near the basement. Finding a screwdriver, he repaired the front door's hinges, making it functional again. Walking back to the couch, he pulled an afghan over Teri and awkwardly tucked her in. She was snoring rhythmically as he let himself out. He twisted the knob back and forth, making sure the door locked behind him.

The two uniformed officers were waiting on the front walk. They looked at him inquisitively. "Nothing to worry about," he told them. "She's a little nuts, but she's no danger to anybody. She's asleep now."

They got in their patrol car and drove away. He returned to his Caprice and sat behind the wheel for a moment. Then he left, too, in the opposite direction.

CHAPTER 22

And Then There Were Three

The phone rang, startling Claire. Sitting up with a jerk, she grabbed it from the end table. The book slid to the floor, and she lost her page. Before answering, she glanced at the screen. Private number.

"Hello?" Claire asked.

"Hello, is this Claire? This is Lola, returning your call."

"Lola! I am so glad you called back. Thea from the Moonshadows store gave me your name. She told me you have gifts, and I am hoping you can share some insight and guidance regarding a situation with a friend."

"What is it exactly that you need help with?"

Claire started out trying to keep it simple, but the story poured out of her. She did not want to forget a single detail.

"Whoa, whoa, whoa. Slow down," Lola said after a minute. "You sound like Lorelai from *Gilmore Girls*, I can't follow along."

Claire's anxiety was replaced by a sudden calm. She was on the right path with the right person. Teri always accused her of talking as fast as Lorelai Gilmore; it was an inside joke between them.

In a slower and calmer voice, Claire started again. Lola stopped her after she mentioned Bellissimo's accusation that she and Teri were in on the whole thing, and the fact that she had seen ectoplasm near Teri.

"It sounds like the spirit may be trying to attach to her and use her to get to you. If so, she's really just a pawn here. Often, those who spirits attach to don't even know that they are carrying the spirits around with them. It tends to present a lot like schizophrenia," Lola said. "What does the spirit want from you? Did he say?"

"I'm thinking he thinks I can somehow prevent him from facing justice on the other side. What do you think?"

"Oh yes. It's certainly not unreasonable, especially given the heinous nature of his actions on this plane."

"So, are you also a medium, then?" Claire asked.

"Yes," Lola replied. "I have it in my blood. My grandparents on both sides of the family were

Native American—my grandfather on my mother's side was a medicine man and always used his intuition and the whispers of the Ancient Ones to guide him.

"I remember my grandmother acting tough and Americanized as she tried to tell me not to worry when I went to her crying about the smoke I kept smelling near Grandpa's chair after he passed on to Summerland," she continued. "'It's just Papa's way of letting us know he is here and watching over us,' she told me. From then on I started talking to him on a regular basis, and he kept me from harm more than once. I talk to my grandmother all the time, too, even though she has been gone from this plane for nearly forty years." There was a hint of nostalgia in Lola's voice that made Claire think of her own mother.

"I remember the first time she came to me after she passed," she continued. "I was taking care of a sick dog and was getting really worried because he'd stopped eating and drinking. I heard Grandma's voice in my head telling me what to do to make him better. I didn't question her, and after that, I just paid attention to the clues I would get—the words I would hear or the smells that floated around me. It was and still is like looking into a room most people don't see.

"After that," Lola concluded, "it was like I had opened a door, and I have never looked back or questioned the information that I have received, as I know it comes from a place of great love."

"Wow," Claire replied. "That is a ton of validation. No wonder you never looked back. I get it. All that we get comes from a place of love. I firmly believe that."

Just then, Claire got a text message from Gia, inviting her to breakfast at the diner at the end of town the next morning.

"Lola, do you know Gia Garviano?" she asked.

"I do."

"Does Gia do mediumship too?"

"No, she is an empath and she does a lot of healing with crystals and Reiki. She is an amazing healer and she is always able to keep people around her grounded," Lola replied.

"Oh, good. Well, she suggested breakfast tomorrow morning. Would that work for you?"

"Yeah, absolutely. Is eleven okay?"

"I think that should be perfect. I'll text Gia back and we can talk more then. Thank you so much; I am extremely grateful. See you tomorrow," Claire said, and ended the call.

She quickly texted Gia the time and then set her phone down and took a deep breath. It felt as though the air in the room was lighter. She no longer felt so overwhelmed by all that she had been carrying. Still, she was a little worried about bringing other people in. She didn't want to put Gia or Lola in danger, after all.

She spent the rest of the evening alternately pacing the floor and reading the book she had gotten at Thea's.

* * *

Pulling into the diner's small parking lot, she parked next to a car with a "Coexist" bumper sticker. *Maybe there are likeminded people I never knew existed around here after all,* she thought as she headed for the entrance.

"How many?" asked the hostess.

"Three, please," Claire answered.

The hostess led her to a large dining area in the back of the building.

"Coffee while you wait?" she asked, handing her a menu.

"That would be great," Claire replied.

"I will tell your waitress," the hostess said and walked away.

Looking up from the menu, Claire saw a young woman carrying a coffeepot walking toward her, with Gia and Lola on her heels.

"Hey, Claire," Lola called from behind. "You've met Gia before, right?"

"Hi Gia!" Claire greeted. "Yes. You taught the crystal healing class, about the use of stones and their properties, right?"

"Yes, that is me!" Gia replied with a deep laugh. "Thea had to jog my memory about you," she continued. "She has an incredible memory for how people have interacted with each other in her so-called tribe of women friends. I can't say that I remember you specifically, but your energy feels familiar." Gia took off a small black cape and settled into the booth, across from Claire and next to Lola.

Both women were studying Claire with great intensity. She knew they were reading her energy, just as she was reading theirs. It was a bit unnerving, but comforting at the same time. Finally, she was with a group of women who were like-minded and from whom she wouldn't have to hide her true self behind the walls she had so carefully built over the years. Walls she kept up even with Teri.

Gia was the first to break the silence. "So you said you were in need of assistance. I'm not sure what you need, but I will try and give you my perspective and insight." Claire felt like Gia wasn't addressing her as much as the swirling spirits she could see hovering above the other woman like a slow-moving people-tornado.

"Thank you. I am so grateful for any help either of you can offer. I would really like any otherworldly assistance you can offer, as well," Claire said.

There was another long moment of silence, during which the three of them noticed that the waitresses were all gathered across the room, chewing gum and staring at them.

Gia winked at them, grinned, then turned her huge brown eyes back to Claire. "I have had a cloudy, foggy head all morning and it feels like I am dizzy," she said. "I don't want to alarm you, but I don't usually get such strong feelings about someone I've never met. This is serious. Whatever is going on with your friend isn't good." She shook her head as if to clear it.

The waitress came back to take their orders, without making eye contact with anyone.

Once she was gone again, Lola looked at Gia and then at Claire. "Gia and I drove in together and we were talking," she said. "We think that there is a lot more going on than you know right now, and we aren't exactly sure what we can do. What are you thinking?"

"I'm not a hundred percent sure," Claire said, looking down into her coffee cup. "I don't know why Christine came to me if she had been gone for so long before she was hit. That just doesn't make sense to me. I don't know why this other jerk chose the train I was going to be on to pull off his big exit plan, and I certainly don't know why Teri was dragged into this," she concluded with a defeated sigh.

The waitress returned with their orders, and no one spoke for a few minutes. They sat with their heads down, moving the food around on their plates and thinking.

"Okay, I will be the first to say it," Gia said. "There is a lot of shit going on here and because of you, your friend is in the middle of it. It isn't like you planned it, but it happened. You know that the lower the vibration, the easier a person is to attach to. No way in hell was that jerk attaching to you, so he latched on to the next best thing. There! It's out now; let's decide what, if anything, we can do to help."

"I agree," Lola said, nodding. "It isn't your fault, but this thing followed *you* and stuck to *her*. I'm not sure what we can do if she doesn't realize, or want to acknowledge, that there is something going on outside of this realm. Or if she will even let us help her."

Claire wasn't sure what to say. She grabbed a big piece of bacon and chewed. "Have you ever opened a portal to the other side?" she finally asked.

Lola and Gia looked at one another and then both shook their heads.

"I learned how a long time ago," Claire said, looking down at her plate. "I have a lot of respect for my teachers, but I'm not sure if I can do it alone. I'm not even sure it will work. But would that be an option you would be willing to help me with?"

Lola and Gia stared at her as they processed the request.

"Hey, Montgomery," a familiar voice boomed from behind Claire. "Your friend flipping out or something?" Bellissimo asked, as he barreled toward their table.

"What are you talking about?" Claire snapped, annoyed.

"There was a noise complaint last night and I recognized the name, so I thought I would swing by and see what was up. Your friend was bouncing off the walls, talking about hearing banging noises in her apartment. Only there *were* no noises, except from her—she had the TV and the stereo running full blast, and it looked like somebody set a bomb off in her apartment. Clothes everywhere, pieces of wood flung all over the place, and dishes piled up to the ceiling. It was like a hoarder's house. When I asked her about you, she flipped out on me. So what's her deal? Is she crazy? Is she a meth-head? What's going on with her?" Bellissimo glared at her.

"I haven't seen her in a few days, but no, she isn't on drugs, and she isn't crazy," Claire responded, controlling her anger and not bothering to introduce him to her companions.

"Well, she's not acting normal," he replied dismissively. "She's just lucky I decided she wasn't a danger to herself or others, or I'd have done more than give her sleeping pills."

Lola and Gia watched as Claire and Bellissimo glared at each other. Even though he was standing, which could have given him a psychological advantage, Claire refused to look away. There was no way she was going to let this asshole think that she was intimidated by his threats, and there was also no way Teri would do any type of drugs.

Finally, he turned to leave. "I know there's something wrong here; I'm telling you I can feel it," he said over his shoulder. "I will find out, trust me. And if I get one more call like last night, your pal is going to be transported to a secure medical facility."

"Wow, that guy's a real asshole," Lola said as she watched him walk out the door.

"Who da hell does he think he is?" Gia asked, in a Brooklyn accent that usually remained tucked away.

"He's a detective. He thinks like a cop," Claire said with an angry shrug. Then she got back to the point. "Listen, I know that you aren't sure what you can do, but Teri must be in trouble if he showed up at her house. Will you help me?"

"Yeah, I'll do what I can," Gia agreed with a nod.

"Me, too," Lola said.

Standing up, Claire reached for her jacket.

"I'm going to call and see if I can get Teri to talk to me before I go to work this afternoon. I will give you two a call after I talk to her," she said, adding, "Breakfast is on me. And thank you both so much for coming." She took her phone out of her coat pocket and walked toward the cash register.

CHAPTER 23

ATTACHING

"Head games! That's all I get from you is head games! And I can't take it anymore! Head games!"

Teri sat bolt upright. She was alone, but the stereo was blaring Foreigner's hit. She jumped to her feet. "No!" she screamed.

She grabbed her car keys and jacket and bolted out the door, still wearing her old, gray fleece slippers. The stereo immediately fell silent as the door slammed shut behind her on its own.

Shivering, she unlocked the car door, jumped inside, and started the engine. She was disoriented, but fully awake. Realizing she'd left her cell inside, she glanced at the house, but she wasn't going back in there. She put the car in drive and peeled out of the driveway.

After two blocks, she looked down at the car stereo screen—it was 9:30 AM.

She continued driving in the direction of town for a good twenty minutes before she felt safe enough to pull over to the side of the road.

Dammit, Claire! What have you done to me?"
she said to herself, shaking her head dejectedly
and looking out the window. A small shop was
directly across the street from where she'd parked.
The name caught her attention. *Moonshadows,* she
murmured. She looked away and stared pensively
down at the steering wheel.

The car's clock read 9:57 AM when Teri pulled
the keys from the ignition. Stepping outside, she
crossed the busy cobblestone street toward the
small building.

She reached for the door handle and at the
same time, Thea pushed it open for her.

"Well, hello there," Thea greeted warmly. "Are
you troubled?"

Teri gave the older woman a suspicious glare
and walked past her into the shop. "I need to contact someone," she said, and then her voice trailed
off as she looked around the room.

"A lot of people need that," Thea said with a
motherly glance, and motioned for Teri to follow
her deeper into the store.

"Who are you looking for?" Thea asked. "Is
this someone you have unresolved issues with?"

"I guess you could say that," Teri answered
stoically.

Thea regarded her for a long moment. "Do you
know whom you are trying to contact, or do you
just want answers to specific questions?"

"I just want answers," Teri replied flatly, chewing on her thumbnail.

"Have you ever contacted spirits before?"

"No," Teri replied, growing agitated. "They seem to be interested in bugging the shit out of me, though."

"I see." Thea glanced up and down the shelves that lined the wall. "I think I have what you need," she said with a nod, motioning for Teri to follow her.

They walked down an aisle along a purple wall. Thea stopped in front of a tall shelf. The smell of sage was thick; Teri recognized it from Claire's place.

Thea grabbed an old box from the topmost corner, looked down at it, and then turned back to Teri.

"Are your intentions good?" she asked, looking deeply into her eyes.

"Of course," Teri answered, immediately grabbing the box from Thea's hands. "I just want to know what's going on."

Teri scanned the box's black and tan cover. *OUIJA*, it said in bold type across the front. Normally she would have laughed at anyone who would suggest getting answers from what appeared to be nothing more than a board game. Things had changed.

"Do you mean harm to anyone?" Thea asked, looking at her more closely.

"Not at all," Teri answered definitively, looking back up at her. She meant it, too. She just wanted this thing out of her house. Out of her head.

Thea continued to study her. "If you have negativity or bad energy toward anyone, this will not help you," she warned. "It can't."

"I am not negative," Teri answered defensively. *I'm about to get negative on this lady if she doesn't get off my ass, though,* she thought. "What do I owe you?" Before Thea could answer, she began walking toward the checkout counter.

Thea stood watching her for a moment. "Dear," she said, as she stepped behind the register. "The dark cannot produce light. This medium can only bring certain answers. For better or worse, your emotions will dictate the rest. Understand this."

"I understand," Teri replied angrily, handing the woman a one-hundred-dollar bill and receiving three twenties and a ten back.

Thea continued talking to her, but Teri wouldn't make eye contact and gripped the Ouija board tightly under her arm. "There are steps you need to follow in order to use this medium safely and effectively," Thea said, pointing toward a shelf of herbs across the room. "I recommend cleansing the board as well as yourself before casting your circle."

"Casting? Circle?" Teri looked at Thea as though she were a lunatic.

"Protection," Thea answered. She shook her head uncomfortably. "I don't think this is what you need after all." With a concerned expression, she reached out to take the board back.

"I'm good," Teri said, pulling away from her and walking quickly out of Moonshadows.

"A thirty-dollar solution...fantastic," Teri muttered, annoyed, as she walked back across the street and got into her car. *Unreal.*

She sat in the car staring back at the shop. The older woman was gazing back at her through the curtains. Catching a sudden chill, Teri shook her head and started the engine.

Clouds were moving in to cover the sun. Teri lit a cigarette and began the drive back home.

Claire does shit like this all the time. It can't be too dangerous; she's crazy, but she's physically fine, Teri reassured herself as she crossed Pickett Avenue, about a mile from her house.

Pulling into her driveway, she stared at her living room windows, which seemed peaceful and quiet. She sat still for a tense moment, her legs feeling heavy. She looked down at the box lying on the passenger seat. Clutching it to her chest, she stepped out of the car and crossed the driveway toward her front door.

She gently pushed the key into the doorknob and slowly opened the door, as quietly as a teenager sneaking home hours past curfew. Her heart raced; sweat trickled down her temples.

The stereo was playing Billy Joel's "Allentown" at a very reasonable volume. She sighed with relief, and set the box on the hallway table while she slipped off her coat and boots. Picking the box up again, she brought it into the living room and laid it gently on the coffee table.

Her cell phone was still in the kitchen where she'd left it. Grabbing it, she sat on the living room couch, pensively chewing her thumbnail. *What in the hell is a protection circle?*, she asked herself. She stared at Claire's number in her contact list for several minutes.

"Nah," she said, dropping the phone beside her. "I'm going to end this shit right now."

The box had a small gold latch on its side. Teri twisted it open and flipped the lid back. Inside lay a simple flat board with the word *OUIJA* scrawled across it.

She studied it. There was a picture of the sun in the upper-left corner, and one of the moon on the upper-right corner. All the letters of the alphabet were printed in an arc across the middle of the board, along with the numbers zero through nine and a few other symbols she wasn't sure of. At the top of the board, toward its center, the words *yes* and *no* appeared. The word *goodbye* appeared at the bottom center. She smirked.

Resting atop the board was a heart-shaped piece of wood with a circular piece of clear glass or crystal in its center. There were no instructions in the box, but it all seemed self-explanatory. Like most people, Teri had seen enough movies to know the basics of using a Ouija board: You held onto the little piece of wood, asked it a question, and your answers would be spelled out.

Teri set the box aside, put the board in the center of the coffee table, and placed the heart-shaped piece of wood in the middle of it. She tucked her hair behind her ears, sat up straight and touched her fingers to the edges of the piece of wood. *Let's do this*, she thought.

She looked up at the ceiling, trying to figure out what to ask.

Her cell rang: "Magic" by Olivia Newton-John, the ringtone she'd assigned Claire. She leaned over, tapped Ignore, and placed her fingers back on the piece of wood. She took a deep, nervous breath.

"Is this the pedophile that was at Claire's house? Is that who's bothering me?" Teri asked aloud. She looked down at her fingers where they rested atop the unmoving piece of wood. She waited, staring at it for about five minutes. Nothing happened. She exhaled in frustration, removed her fingers, and stormed out to the kitchen.

Throwing open an oak-faced cabinet, she pulled out a large bottle of Cabernet and a beer stein. *Buncha bullshit*, she muttered as she unscrewed the cap and filled the stein. She took a quick drink, and then froze. The heart-shaped piece of wood was sitting in front of her on the kitchen table. Her hands shook violently, and she put the stein down quickly before she dropped it.

She turned her back on the table, reached behind her for the stein, and drank the whole thing in one long, panicked gulp. When she turned around, the piece of wood was gone. The house was silent.

She glanced out into the living room and saw the piece of wood where she'd left it, atop the Ouija board. She slowly sat down at the table, tears forming in her eyes. She poured herself another full mug of wine, took a drink, and took another look in the living room. Everything was quiet and undisturbed. *You're losing it,* she thought. *Get it together.* She sighed and stood up.

With slow, deliberate steps, she approached the board, mug of wine in hand. She took another long drink and sat back down on the couch in front of the board.

Setting the mug on the table next to it, she rubbed her hands back and forth nervously on her thighs and then softly touched the piece of wood with her fingertips.

She tilted her head down, regarding it contemplatively for a moment.

"Is anyone there?" she asked, raising her eyebrows.

Nothing.

She chewed her bottom lip, staring at the unmoving piece of wood.

Teri picked up her mug and took another drink. She wiped her mouth on her sleeve, put her fingers back on the piece of wood, and then lost it. "What the fuck is your problem?" she yelled.

Her eyes widened as the piece of wood started to move violently in a circle around the board on its own, dragging her hands with it, and then abruptly situated the crystal circle in its center over the letter Y. Then it flew to the letter O, then darted over to U.

Teri flew backward on the couch, eyes wide.

The piece of wood sat still in the center of the board. She stared at it for several minutes.

Cautiously, she sat back up and gently touched it again. "I don't understand," Teri whispered. "Why are you upset with me?"

The piece of wood slowly spelled out the word *p-a-w-n*, and then stopped.

"What's a pawn?" Teri asked, fingers resting gently on its side.

No answer. Teri furrowed her brow. "I'm a pawn?" she asked.

The piece of wood perched over the word *yes*.

She grabbed the mug of wine and finished the last of it, fully buzzed now.

She leaned forward again and placed her fingers back on the piece of wood. Before she could form her question, it began to move.

Teri watched, terrified, as it slowly spelled out: *You must die.*

"Fuck you!" She leapt up from the couch, flipping the board over and throwing it across the room. Breathing heavily, and suddenly light-headed, she stared at it where it lay upside down on the floor.

A moment later there was a loud knock on the wall next to her. The hair on her arms stood up. Terrified, she closed her eyes tightly and lay on the couch, curled into a ball.

Her entire body shook with fear. Disoriented, she tried to stand up, but her legs and arms felt like noodles; all of her strength was gone. She could feel herself fading into unconsciousness, and beginning to panic, at the same time. Mercifully, she passed out.

"Thaaaaat's right," a low-toned male voice, almost a growl, whispered.

A moment later the board and the small piece of wood slowly began to slide on their own across the floor, coming to rest next to the box they had arrived in.

CHAPTER 24

THE CIRCLE

Claire glanced back at Lola and Gia while the cashier rang her up. "Thank you again," she called out to her new friends as she headed for the door.

"Keep us posted," Gia called.

"I'm off today, too, if you need any help," Lola added.

The drive to Teri's wasn't a long one, but it gave Claire enough time to imagine all kinds of terrifying possibilities.

The two of them had never gone this long without speaking, and although she knew her friend was pissed, the emotional distance Teri was creating seemed so out of character that Claire couldn't stop the "what-if"s from bouncing around her brain. The whole situation was too personal; she couldn't focus well enough to allow her gifts, as witch or medium, to give her the answers she needed.

She pulled up in front of Teri's house and sat staring at the front door for a long time before daring to knock. There was no answer. Claire looked at the lawn and a chill raced through her body. The faint images of their snow angels were still there, but one had become much larger and had two black rocks where its eyes would have been. She descended to the lawn and took a closer look. Someone had also added a smile with teeth that a dog had apparently pissed on.

She banged on the door again. Teri's car was in the driveway, but there was still no response. She bent over the border stones that protected the flower bed. Digging under the snow, she found the rock on which Teri had painted a sunflower and hoped the spare key was still there. It was. Claire grabbed it, headed back up the steps, and shoved it into the lock.

Before opening the door, a putrid smell filled her nostrils.

"I know you are here," she shouted. "Where are you?" Claire passed the couch and saw piles of clothes flung everywhere. As she explored the house, the mess shocked her. The clothes and newspapers, usually confined to the couch, were strewn up and down the hallway. The small table under the mirror just outside of Teri's bedroom was tipped over and two pairs of pants had been hung across the mirror, hiding it.

She had to shove the bedroom door open with all her strength. Drawers yawned open and all of Teri's belongings were piled on the floor and across the bed.

"Teri, are you in here?" Claire called out, becoming more anxious by the second.

She couldn't tell if Teri was under one of the piles or not. Walking around the bed, she patted it down, reaching across the entire mattress and finally pulling off the covers. Empty.

"Teri. Where are you?" Claire asked, her heart pounding as she sat on the edge of the bed. Panic was starting to take over and worst-case scenarios were racing through her mind. She knocked twice on the bathroom door and held her breath as she opened it.

Teri was lying motionless in the tub. Claire's eyes began to sting with tears as she raced over to her friend. Bending over, she reached into the water. It was still warm. Suddenly, Teri's eyes popped open and she bolted upright. Shocked, Claire jumped backward, slipping on the bath mat and knocking her head sharply against the towel rack on the wall.

"What the fuck are you doing?" Teri yelled, ripping her earbuds out. She stood up and fumbled for her towel.

Claire was rubbing the back of her head, which was throbbing with pain. "Why the hell didn't you answer me? I've been frantic looking for you. Your house looks like a bomb hit it and you haven't been taking my calls!" she yelled.

"Yeah, well, because of you I can't sleep anymore!" Teri shot back. "There are noises and all kinds of weird shit happening. This is the only place I feel comfortable and I dozed off!" Her eyes were swollen and red with frustration.

Grabbing her robe from the back of the door, she glared at Claire. "Do you mind if I fucking get dressed?" she hissed.

"I'll wait for you in the living room," Claire replied, shaking.

Pushing the button on Teri's coffee maker, she began to move dirty dishes out of the sink, then changed her mind. Filling the basin with hot water and half a bottle of dish soap, she put them back in to soak.

Walking to the living room, she started to sort and fold Teri's clothes. It was at that moment she realized how much like her mother and her nana she was. Mundane tasks helped to clear her mind and allowed her to receive helpful guidance from the other side, without her conscious mind getting in the way and trying too hard to interpret the messages' meaning or direction.

Teri eventually emerged, fully dressed. She looked exhausted. There were bags under her bloodshot eyes, her skin was pasty white and her hair looked like a blind bird's nest.

"What's going on with you?" Claire asked, almost in a whisper.

"You tell me!" Teri snapped. "I don't know what you did with those shrubs you're always burning or the screwed-up stories you tell, but this is messed up and I am sick of it."

"Listen, I told you that the guy I hit on the tracks was dark," Claire said as she led Teri to a stool in the kitchen.

Popping a coffee pod into the machine, Claire fished a mug from the soapy water. She rinsed it, dried it with a paper towel, and placed it on the coffee maker's platform, pushing the brew button. She was stalling before broaching the subject of Lola and Gia, and how they were going to help her get rid of the spirit that was tormenting Teri.

"Listen, I know that you don't believe in a lot of what I do. But I can see how you're suffering, and would like to do a circle to cross this guy over and help us to get back to normal," she offered.

"What do you mean 'a circle'? And what do you mean 'cross this guy over'? What does it have to do with *me*?" Teri sneered.

"He is attached to you now. He is using you," Claire said as she looked directly into her friend's eyes. "Listen, I know this isn't easy for you to accept, but I also know that *you* know something isn't right. Otherwise you wouldn't be sleeping in your bathtub. The thing is, he's wearing you down. And the more worn-down you are, the easier it is for him to stay attached and to eventually take over."

Teri nodded her head, exhausted, and sat quietly. "So what would you do?" she asked.

"I want to get Lola and Gia, two friends of mine who are both…like-minded people…to help me cast a protective circle and then open a portal to cross this guy over and away from you," Claire explained.

"You know what? Fine," Teri said after a moment. "I still don't really believe this shit is what you say it is, but I need sleep." She didn't tell Claire about the Ouija board, which was now buried behind a pile of old magazines in the farthest corner of the living room.

"Great. Let me make a couple of phone calls while you go fix your hair," Claire said. She grabbed Teri's hand and helped her off the stool, turning her toward the hall and giving her shoulders a slight push.

She called Lola and Gia and they agreed to meet her and Teri on Muir's Mountain at two o'clock. They said they would come in one car and would bring some Magickal tools with them and plenty of sage and cedar to burn.

* * *

The ride to Muir's Mountain was a quiet one. Teri wasn't completely on board with the plan and was still pretty pissed off at Claire. She'd even insisted on driving her own car to the meeting. Claire was very apprehensive about letting Teri know just how dangerous the entity she carried with her was. She kept scratching her scar and checking her rearview mirror to ensure that Teri was still following her.

About ten minutes to two, Claire and Teri arrived at the empty space that had once been 421 Milton Springs Road. A small, lime-green car followed them into what had once been a driveway and parked behind them.

"Hello, ladies, thank you so much for coming," Claire called to Gia and Lola. Everyone was introduced, and they brought all their tools to a clearing about fifty feet away, where she guessed the house must have stood before the hurricane hit. Teri followed, wary and observant, saying nothing.

Claire led the way through the deep snow. The others followed, stepping into her boot prints so they wouldn't sink up to their knees.

"Does this look good?" Claire asked Gia over her shoulder.

"Yeah, dis will work," Gia said in her thick Brooklyn accent.

"Yup, this will be just fine," Lola agreed. She began rooting around in an enormous, green canvas duffel bag. Pulling out a compass and a nine-foot piece of clothesline rope, she cleared a spot and put the bag down. It would serve as an anchor so she could outline where the circle and the elements should be placed.

"Hey, Teri, come stand right here, will you?" Lola said. It wasn't really a question.

"What for?" Teri asked.

"Because you are gonna clear the snow from this little area so we can use it as the North direction," Lola said and walked forward, clothesline in one hand and compass in the other.

"Gia, can you take East," Lola said, again making it more a statement than a question.

Gia nodded and moved into position.

"Claire, I want you to clear out South," Lola said, marking an X in the snow with her glove before moving on to the final spot. "I'll take care of West," she concluded, tucking the compass away in her pocket and dropping the cord to scoop snow with her hands.

Once all four directions were clear of snow, Claire, Lola, and Gia took tools from the green bag, removing an oversized chessboard made of oak and placing it on a waist-high table they'd haphazardly sculpted from the snow that had been cleared from the surrounding area. Claire placed two candles in the snow near the chessboard, one for the God and one for the Goddess, along with one of those big grill lighters and a Peyton that would be used to call the Ancient Ones to the circle.

She placed a small container of spring water in the snow, ready to be used to fill the chalice (the symbol for female) sitting there, and set an Athame (the symbol for male) beside it.

Claire surrounded the chessboard with quartzes to help intensify the power of the circle and the connection to the Ancient Ones, as they would need all the help they could get if the ritual were to succeed.

"Are you ready?" she asked Teri.

"We are all here for you," Gia added.

Lola nodded her head in agreement. "Yup, we are all here. Gia will sweep the circle clear of any lingering energy, and then we will have you stand here by the altar and the three of us will cast the circle and call the quarters..."

"Wait, wait, wait," Teri said, waving her hands and cutting Lola off. "Okay, I have been standing here watching you guys run around in the snow making places for these objects and then set up a chessboard. Really, what the hell do you think you are going to be doing here? Playing a game while you tell me some jerk is attached to me?" Teri was becoming angrier by the second.

"Clearly you're irritated, but that's because he doesn't want you to do this," Gia said.

"You're trying to tell me I don't know what I think?" Teri shot back, and then glared at Claire. "Claire, explain to me again what the fuck this circle thing does?" she hissed.

"Okay," Claire replied calmly, "We are going to make a circle after we sweep out any negative energy that isn't in our highest and best good, making sure that everything we do is correct for this situation."

"I heard that part, but what are you really doing, and what does the Majick part mean?" Teri asked, her voice rising.

"Well, I am going to take that wand, the one in my car that I always tell you not to touch, and envision a stream of protective energy and flow it through myself to create a sacred place where all is correct. I am then going to call in dragons that keep watch over the elements like watchtowers and ask for their help, and ask that they use the gifts that they possess to protect us," Claire replied. Teri stared at her blankly; she continued.

"Then we are going to call in the Ancient Ones. We will pour some water into the chalice and stir it with the Athame and offer them libation before we cut open a hole in the circle and create a one-way portal. We will then ask anyone that is associated with Wayne Douglas Daniels to come forward into the circle and help him to the other side by showing him the light and the love over there," Claire explained, finally stopping and taking a deep breath.

Teri stared at the ground. The three women stood in silence watching her. Several minutes passed before she looked back up.

"Screw you. Screw you, and…screw you too!" Teri shook her head and looked at each woman in turn. "You're all nuts," she said and began to back away from them.

"No, really, we are here to help you," Lola said, taking a step toward Teri.

"I know dat it sounds crazy, but it *is* true," Gia chimed in, also taking a slow step forward.

"Come on, you know you haven't been yourself," Claire said. "I told you that this guy, entity, thing…was a piece of shit and I told you he attached to you. I just want to make sure that you are safe. You know that I wouldn't lie to you. You know that I only have your best interests and welfare at heart. Your mother is worried about you, too," she offered and then she, too, took a step toward Teri.

"Leave my mother out of this," Teri said, retreating further and looking at the three of them fearfully.

Claire, Lola, and Gia exchanged glances.

"Okay, what if we call to the other side and ask for…" Gia began.

"There you go again!" Teri shouted.

Suddenly all three women closed their eyes at the same time and, with their palms upright, silently raised their hands in unison.

Teri narrowed her eyes, watching them for a long moment before breaking the silence.

"You aren't saying anything, but I know you're doing something. What are you conjuring up now? A dead body guard?" She glared at Claire again. "You made me think that all that stuff Karen said was true. You had me believing that my mother really came with a message for me. I actually believed you, and now here I am on the verge of mental breakdown and you and your band of wizards or fairies, or whatever the hell they are, are going to be making invisible circles and calling dragons." She paused, looking at the three of them with disgust. "I hate to break it to you, but dragons only exist on TV. This is bullshit."

Teri turned and ran down the hill to her car. The roar of the motor broke the silence, followed by the squeal of tires as she took off. Claire wanted to run after her, but Gia laid a hand on her shoulder and stopped her.

"Let her go. She isn't ready. He has a hold on her that is just strong enough to keep her from trusting you," Gia said, shaking her head.

"Let's do what we can, since we are here," Lola said. She turned to face the circle and walked toward the makeshift altar.

Claire picked up the broom and made a sweeping motion as she went around the circle clockwise.

Gia, who had been waiting for Claire to finish, walked in from the North and, with the wand in her left hand, started to walk around the circle herself.

"I cast this circle to protect us from all negative energies that may come to do us harm," she said as she walked around the circle in the tracks that Lola had made earlier.

She performed the ritual a second time in silence, nodding her head at each of the directions.

"This circle has been cast and will provide protection for our Majickal workings," Gia called out to the universe on her third time around.

Walking back to the center to join Lola and Claire, Gia pulled a small brown bottle from her jacket pocket. It was filled with a special blend of oil she had picked up in Salem, Massachusetts, when she had gone for Samhain in October.

She uncapped the bottle and tipped it onto her right index finger, then drew a pentagram on her left wrist. She repeated the process with her left index finger and right wrist, and followed that by drawing two more on her forehead and the back of her neck.

She tipped the bottle again to reload her index finger and anointed Lola's wrists, forehead, and the back of her neck before passing the vial to Lola so she could anoint Claire.

Once they all were anointed, Claire walked to the North and raised a small saucer filled with stones and salt toward the sky in her left hand, with her back to her friends. They, too, raised their left arms and with palms up they looked skyward as she began to speak.

"I call upon the element of earth to join us in our circle and share with us your gift of grounding that will offer us sure footing as we do our Majick. Hail and welcome to our circle," Claire said, bowing her head and placing the rocks on the snowy patch of ground that had been cleared earlier.

Lola was next. She walked clockwise to the East position and raised her hand, holding a hand full of feathers. Both Claire, still in the North, and Gia, standing at the altar turned toward the East, raised their left arms into the air, palms held high to the sky.

"I call upon the East and the element of air to help breathe intelligence and knowledge into our Majick. Hail and welcome," Lola said, bowing her head and placing the feathers on the ground in the East just as the wind whipped up and a gust blew them skyward.

Gia took her cue and walked clockwise past both Claire and Lola, stopping in the South, where she took a small votive candle in a glass holder and lifted it upward.

"I call upon the element of fire, the great element of change and cleansing, to join us and assist us with our Majick tonight. Hail and welcome," Gia said with her hand and eyes skyward.

All three walked clockwise toward the West. When they were all in place, they raised their left hands toward the sky, clenching handfuls of snow.

"We call to the West and the power of water to join us and share with us your powerful gift of emotions and transformation," said Lola.

"You are able to nourish crops as you gently fall from the sky, and rip houses from their foundations with your powerful currents," Gia said.

"You can freeze hard and keep others out or thaw and be the water of life. We welcome you to our circle. Hail and welcome," Claire said.

All three walked back to the chessboard, which was covered in a light snow that had begun to fall.

Gia poured water into the chalice until it reached just under the rim. Raising the chalice, she turned to Claire, who was holding the Athame.

"I stir the waters of life," Claire said and plunged the blade into the chalice to stir the water.

Removing the Athame and placing it on the altar, all three women raised the chalice toward the heavens together.

"A libation to the Ancient Ones. We honor you," they chanted in unison.

Claire pulled out a piece of parchment. It contained a spell asking protection for Teri; it invoked Hekate, the goddess of the crossroads, asking her to keep an eye on Teri until this madness was over. Lighting a corner of the parchment paper, she turned it several times until the flames engulfed nearly the entire sheet before letting it float out of her hands so the final corner could burn.

As the paper burned, a feeling of calm and comfort enveloped Lola and Gia. They knew the feeling came from those on the other side, who were giving them a metaphysical hug and letting them know they were there. They would be watching and helping to guide the way, without influencing the free will of those involved.

The flames had consumed the entire spell except for one perfect, triangular section. The three women looked at it, troubled, and then Claire let the piece slip from her fingers and they watched in silence as it floated up into the sky.

"I send this spell out to the cosmos to do my bidding. So mote it be," Claire said uneasily as she turned to look at her friends.

Without Teri present, they had done all that they could for now. Still, Claire wasn't happy. She smelled something waft by her in the air, and she knew it wasn't burnt toast.

All three women walked clockwise around the circle back to the North, raised their right arms, and released the element of water, offering thanks for the power and the gifts that they had shared.

Traveling counterclockwise around the circle, the women released each of the directions and thanked them for their help and their gifts, ending with the North element.

Once they had released all of the elements properly, Gia grabbed the wand and walked counterclockwise again.

"This circle is undone but never broken. May the Majick that we created continue for the good of all, harming none. So mote it be. Merry meet, merry part, and merry meet again," Gia said, walking to the chessboard to tap it three times with the tip of her wand, signaling the end of the ritual.

"Thank you both so much for helping out. I really appreciate your support," Claire said uneasily.

"You are welcome. I know it can't be easy. We are both here if you need us," Lola replied as she looked at Gia nervously. In that moment, Claire knew that they had smelled it, too.

"Lola is right," Gia said. "We are here for you. I think, if you are open to it, that maybe we should ask Thea for her thoughts. I know that she has had some experience with this type of thing, and it is one of the reasons she stepped away from Majick." The women worked together, picking up the tools and knocking down the snow they had piled up to create the altar.

Once everything was cleaned up, they packed all of the tools into the trunk of Lola's car and piled into their cold vehicles for the trip back to St. Albans.

Claire was lost in thought as she drove down the mountain. Classic rock played in the background, but when she hit the edge of town it became so filled with static that she pressed the seek button to find a different station.

"Woo-hoo, witchy woman," the Eagles sang, with perfect clarity and at a much greater volume than what she'd been listening to before. She quickly trained her gaze on the icy road ahead as she felt the car wheels slip. Something was coming. Something bad.

CHAPTER 25

FAIR WARNING

Teri sat in the crew room, silently staring up at the forty-two-inch TV screen on the wall. Dave, a conductor she had worked with for seventeen years, spoke in a whisper with two other railroad workers, Mark and Phil, in the hallway. Each of them took turns peering in at her as she sat on one of the green cushioned chairs surrounding the long metal table. There was no expression on her face.

"Something's wrong with her," one of the men commented.

Dave shook his head, annoyed by the clandestine nature of the conversation. He walked into the crew room, plopped down on a chair across from her, and nonchalantly picked up the *St. Albans Messenger* that was sitting on the table. Teri continued to stare blankly at the TV.

"Hey, Teri," he said. "What's up?"

Teri slowly turned her head and looked directly at him. Something about her gaze was unnerving.

"Nothing, David," she replied curtly, staring dead into his eyes, her pupils appearing unnaturally large.

Dave stood up and slowly walked back out to the hallway, where the other two men were still standing.

"You're right," he said with a shrug, entering the men's locker room. "She's pissed off at someone for sure. Glad it's not me."

Mark and Phil raised their eyebrows at each other, then walked into the crew room and sat quietly a few seats away from Teri, keeping their eyes on the TV screen.

Unable to bear the silence, Mark was the first to speak. "What's wrong, Teri?" he asked with a nervous grin, the florescent light above him flickering like a strobe on his bald head. "You on the rag?"

Teri stood up from the table as though she hadn't heard him and took a step toward the door. She stopped in front of his chair, gazing down at him blankly for a moment, then left the room.

When she was gone, Mark glanced over at Phil, the engineer. "Wow," Phil said with a chuckle, picking up the newspaper and flipping to the sports section. "Thanks a lot. She's my conductor on the yard job tonight."

"Man," Mark said, grimacing, "Whatever that is has nothing to do with me."

Both men laughed.

The yardmaster's voice boomed through the gray metal PA box on the wall.

"Teri? Teri down there?"

Phil stood up, walked over and flipped the call switch down. "Yeah, Jim, she's around here someplace."

"Good," came the reply. "I need you two to go get 442's equipment from the shop and pull it down to the station onto departure track four."

"Four, roger that," Phil replied and walked out into the bluish-gray, cement-blocked hallway. There was no one around. He sighed and walked to the end of the hall, heading for the ladies' locker room. He knocked three times loudly on the door. No answer.

"Hey, Ter," Phil called through the door. "When you're ready, we have to bring 442's equipment down to the station."

Silence.

Phil sighed and returned to the crew room. Mark looked up at him, a questioning look on his face. Phil shrugged as he put on his heavy jacket, safety glasses, and gloves.

"Tell her I'm walking out to the shop when you see her," he said, and then headed into the frigid evening air. The wind whipped the door shut with a howl.

Mark turned the TV off and began to skim the paper Dave had been reading. Hearing a loud, slow, crunching sound, he spun around in his seat, startled. Teri was standing directly behind his chair, chewing on something hard. Jordan almond? Ice cube? Whatever it was, he didn't like the way she was doing it, nor the way she was blankly staring at him. Her large black pupils seemed to be devouring him with each crunch.

"Phil said to tell you he's walking over to the shop, he left a couple minutes ago," Mark said, leaning away from her uncomfortably.

Teri turned around and walked outside. No coat. No gloves. No hat.

Mark stood up and looked out the window. Conditions were now blizzard-like and although only a few seconds had passed, he could barely see Teri as she slowly walked down the tracks toward the shop in the darkness.

* * *

Teri felt her hands begin to sting. She raised them to her face and looked at them, confused. It was as though she had awakened in the middle of a dream. She stopped walking and looked around her as the wind swirled her hair around, whipping her face. She was in the middle of the departure yard.

Blowing warm breath between her cupped, freezing fingers, she turned and looked back toward the crew room, now a few hundred feet away. Then she looked in the direction she had been walking. In the distance, through the darkness and falling snow, she could barely make out the light of a train sitting near the entrance to the shop.

She looked down at her boots and then, conflicted, back toward the train idling in the distance. Her entire body felt like a thousand tiny needles were stabbing it, and her eyes were flooded with tears, which were freezing on her cheeks.

She looked back to the crew room once more and then continued walking toward the light. Crunch…crunch…crunch… she listened to her boots crash through the ice and snow, lulling her back to another place, entranced.

As she drew near the engine, Phil swung open the fireman's-side door and yelled down to her. "Where the hell is your jacket? Are you nuts?"

Teri continued unfazed, past the engine toward the body of the train.

Phil closed the door and stared at her through the engine's side mirror. As he watched her disappear up the trap stairs and into the rear coach, he shook his head and took the radio mic off the engine's console.

"Yard engineer to the yard conductor, over," he called out, checking the mirror again. He sighed with relief when Teri's voice came over the radio.

"Yard conductor answering the yard engineer; ready for the brake test, over."

"Roger that," Phil replied and released the train brakes, pulling the metal handle located right of center on the console.

"Conductor is positioned on the ground at the rear of the consist, okay to set your brakes," Teri said mechanically into the radio.

"Setting the brakes," Phil replied as he pushed the automatic brake handle away from himself toward the windshield.

There was another moment of silence as Teri watched the rear wheel as the brake shoe pressed up against it. "Okay to release the brakes," Teri called out.

Phil immediately put the brake handle in the release position. "Releasing the brakes," he responded.

Teri climbed up the trap stairs into the coaches and lifted her radio back up. "Yard conductor to the yard engineer. We have a good class-two brake test, I'm back onboard and buttoned up, okay to proceed into the station, track number four, signal indication."

Phil nodded to himself and pulled the throttle back, and the train slowly began to move as he stared down at the low-positioned, bright-green flashing signal on the ground in front of him. "We have a limited clear on the signal, lined for track four, out," he called out.

"Limited clear, all lined up for four, roger that," Teri repeated.

The train picked up speed for a moment, and then slowed abruptly as the engineer picked the radio mic back up off the console and released the brakes again, and the train continued to roll.

"Yard engineer to the yard conductor. Good on the running brake test," he called out.

"Roger that, good on the running brake test," she repeated, and then the radio went silent. The train made its way through a series of automatic crossovers and into the station.

A few minutes later the train began a slow crawl as it pulled up alongside the high platform. Teri opened the rear coach door and stood looking out as they came to a stop with all five of the coach's doors on the platform. She stepped onto the yellow safety line and walked down the platform toward the engine to head back to the crew room. Phil met her halfway.

"Hey," he said with a concerned look, breathing heavily in the blustering cold. "I shouldn't have spoken to you that way, but you have to be freezing to death, kiddo."

Teri stared into his eyes for a moment and continued walking. "I figured Jim was in a hurry to get the set down here," she replied stoically.

"Well, screw him!" Phil said protectively. "I don't care how much time you need, you take it," he huffed.

Teri nodded, and without another word, they reached the crew room. Phil held the door open and Teri walked inside.

Mark glanced at them as they entered. Phil gave him a bewildered look. Teri continued down the hall to the ladies' locker room in silence.

A few minutes later the outside door flew open, crashing against the wall. Claire, covered in snow, slammed it closed again behind her.

She stomped the snow off her boots, unwrapped a wool scarf from her face and removed her hat and gloves. She took a deep breath, noting the silence, and then walked into the crew room where Mark and Phil sat. Mark and Phil waved at her and went back to reading their newspapers.

"Quiet in here tonight," Claire said, standing in the doorway.

"You could say that," Phil said with a shrug.

"Anything going on tonight?" she asked.

Mark looked at Phil.

"Just one hell of a cold night tonight," Phil said, glancing back at Mark. "But whaddaya going to do, you know," he concluded, raising his eyebrows.

"Anyone else here, or is it just the two of you?" she asked anxiously.

"Are you looking for someone in particular?" he asked, annoyed.

Claire could sense that he was getting agitated. "Nah, just curious, you guys have a great night."

She gave them a slight smile, turned on her heel and headed toward the ladies' locker room. She slowly opened the door and peered inside.

"Anyone here?" she called into the room, which was lined with three rows of pale-blue lockers. She walked slowly around the corner to the three bathroom stalls and silently bent down and looked underneath them. No one was there.

She stood up and flipped her hair back and turned toward the rows of lockers. She quietly walked around each row. No one was there, either. She sighed and sat down on the long wooden bench that lined the wall. *Her car's here,* she said to herself, and stood up again.

The only other place Teri could reasonably be was up in the yardmaster's office. She walked back down the hall to the door that led upstairs. The stairwell was dark and she couldn't hear anyone talking as she reached the second floor landing.

She looked into the yardmaster's office, which consisted of a huge window overlooking the entire yard and station tracks. A sophisticated screen sat just above the windows, showing the signal system electronically and indicating where the different trains were located within a twenty-mile radius, as well as whether they were stopped, where, and so on. In the evening, the room was always dark to enhance the yardmaster's vision of the yard and screen. There was also a large control board for radio contact with everyone from the crews to the dispatchers to management to emergency personnel.

"Hey, Jim," Claire said with a smile.

Jim spun around on his seat. "Hey, Claire, how are you doing? Have a seat," he offered, motioning toward a rolling chair with a tired grin.

Claire smiled and shook her head. "Hey, have you seen Teri around?" she asked pensively.

Jim's face brightened. "Yeah, she just brought 442's equipment down with Phil, she's down there somewhere."

Claire thanked him and left the office.

"Have a great night," Jim called after her. "And stay warm, it's friggin' freezing out there."

"Tell me about it!" Claire yelled back. "I've got three layers on now and it's not enough."

"Where are you hiding?" she whispered as she reached the bottom of the staircase.

She walked back to the crew room and stood in the doorway. "Where's Teri?" she asked Phil.

"Hopefully out buying herself a jacket, how the hell do I know?" he grumbled.

Claire rolled her eyes and bundled up again, wrapping her face in the heavy, white wool scarf her mom had knitted for her just before she passed. She opened the door to the outside, careful to keep a firm hold on it this time, and stepped out into the darkened train yard. The red stop signals glowed through the darkness, giving the area an eerie reddish aura.

She walked toward the secure gate leading out to the employee parking lot, shivering. She caught something in her peripheral vision and spun to her right, looking toward the station tracks and the red signals marking their end. No one was there. Claire opened the gates and began to trudge toward the parking lot.

Teri, watching in the darkness, stepped out from behind the glowing red signal, sat on top of it, and lit a cigarette. She slowly blew the smoke out as she watched Claire walk to her car.

"Idiot," she sneered with a guttural man's laugh. She hopped off the signal just as Claire pulled out of the station parking lot. With a wide grin, she began walking back to the crew room.

She took a seat on a bench covering the length of the hallway. She sat still, staring straight ahead with her back pressed against the wall.

The yardmaster's voice boomed over the PA and Teri smiled and slowly turned her head in the direction of the box.

"Teri? You down there?"

Teri stood up and began to walk back toward the crew room. She came face to face with Phil, who was about to answer Jim.

"Sit down," Teri said flatly.

Phil made a shitty face but retreated to the table. Teri flipped down the call button.

"Yeah, Jim," she called.

"Hold on a second, Teri, I'll get right back with you, I have to make a call."

"Roger that," Teri replied and let go of the switch. She stood, staring blankly, as Mark and Phil watched her.

* * *

"Hey, Jim, didn't I just leave there?" Claire asked with a laugh, answering the call as she drove.

"Hi," Jim said with a chuckle. "I'm sorry, Claire, but 397's engine died and the crew has run out of time under the hours of service law. I need to keep Phil here for the equipment turns. Any chance I can con you into taking 442's equipment down to Arkcliffe to tie onto them and tow them back up here?"

Claire looked at the dashboard clock.

"Look," Jim began. "You can go track speed, I'll give you a whole set so it doesn't take forever like it would if I sent a single engine. I don't mind at all, I'm just in a bind here. Six-seventy-six and 922 are due in soon. I'm going to have a mess here if I can't keep Phil to turn them in the yard to return to the city tonight. I already have a conductor I'm going to send out ahead of you, so when you get there you can just tie onto them and come right back up. An hour and a half, tops," he pleaded.

Claire rubbed her forehead as she looked out at the blowing snow. Jim waited quietly for her to respond. She knew if she said no, the passengers and equipment would be sitting there for at least three and a half more hours before being rescued and brought back to the station.

"Claire," Jim finally said, "Congress doesn't take this long."

"Did you clear it with the Local?" she asked, still hoping to find a way to say no.

"Yup, I explained to the Local chairman and he agreed that the passengers and crew needed to get into the station as quickly as possible to avoid losing heat or running out of water for the toilets and the café. He is just going to have the next guy in line time-slip you to make up for losing his turn on the list."

"Okay, give me a few minutes to grab a bite and a coffee and I'll take it. You owe me," Claire said and eased into the left lane to make a U-turn.

"Yup, I do. Thank you," Jim said.

"Does the conductor you're sending have the paperwork?"

"Yes. Yes. I'll make sure everything's in order. Just come in, your bulletins and the equipment will be on track four, waiting."

"I'll be back in a half-hour," Claire said reluctantly and ended the call before Jim could begin his thank-you speech.

"Where the *hell* is she?" Claire said aloud as she pulled into a fast-food drive-through. She rolled her window down and a cheerful teenager greeted her through the intercom, which was adorned with a picture of a cup of chili.

"Welcome to Dig's! Would you like to try our two-for-two cheeseburger special?" she asked.

"No, thank you," Claire answered quickly. "Can I have a classic burger and a large coffee, black, please?"

"Would you like fries with that?"

Claire felt a waft of frigid air blow in through the window and a faint light began to materialize before her inside the car. It was a spirit. She sat in silence as the car seemed to disappear and the figure took shape before her.

"Christine?" Claire murmured, gazing at the light that surrounded the girl.

"Yes," she answered softly. "Don't go," she said. Her voice and silhouette began to fade as she repeated, "Don't go."

"I'm here," Claire replied reassuringly. "I'm here for you."

"Little John!" Christine's spirit exclaimed in the happiest voice Claire had ever heard her use. "He is here, here now." Her voice was becoming a whisper and Claire strained to hear her.

"He's with you?" she asked desperately. She could see a small figure beside Christine. The specter slowly nodded, smiling, and both of them began to disappear.

"Don't go…" were the last words Claire could make out; then she heard a loud mechanical voice.

"Ma'am, are you there? Do you want fries or not?" the teenager repeated, pulling Claire back into the moment.

Claire started to pant and lose her patience. *Please let her stop talking,* she said to herself as she pressed the button back in, trying to process what had just transpired.

"Just what I ordered, please," she said, running her fingers through her hair.

"Okay, coming right up," the girl said cheerfully. "Two dollars and ninety-seven cents is your total, ma'am, please pull up to the second window."

Claire handed the pony-tailed blonde a five-dollar bill. The girl smiled at her and passed her the coffee and burger, followed by her change.

* * *

Jim's voice came over the PA. "Teri, please come up here."

Teri headed out the crew room door to the stairwell. She climbed the stairs slowly, one at a time. Jim spun around, startled to find her directly behind him. "Cripes!" he yelled with a laugh. "Don't scare me like that!"

Teri stared down at him, her expression blank. Jim noticed a strange quality about her eyes; he couldn't define it.

"Take the company vehicle down to Arkcliffe," he said, tossing her the keys from his desk drawer. Teri caught them in her left hand. "The engine on 397 shit the bed and the crew outlawed. I need you to go down there, tie 442's equipment onto it, and tow it back up here. We're not sending a single engine, so it'll be track speed. Claire is going to bring the equipment down to you."

"She's going to be coming at track speed?" Teri asked, eyes gleaming in the darkened room.

"One hundred and ten miles per hour, track speed," he confirmed with a nod.

Teri took the keys out of her pocket, smiled, and then looked back up at him. "Anything else?" she asked.

"Yeah, make sure you have Claire's set of orders as well."

Teri flipped the keys around in a circle on her finger as she turned to walk away. "She's all done," Teri said and then stopped short. "She's all set." She gave Jim a thumbs-up and a wide grin and descended the stairs to the crew-room level. She walked past Mark and Phil, watching TV together, and then outside. Teri looked through the blustering snow at her wristwatch and started to walk toward the employee parking lot.

* * *

Claire turned her wipers to a higher speed and leaned closer to the windshield, straining to see the road. "Why did I let myself get talked into this?" she grumbled, keeping her eyes on the road ahead and grabbing the coffee out of the console.

She felt something stuck to the side of the Styrofoam cup and picked at it with her thumb as she drove. Becoming annoyed, she tore it off, along with the bottom portion of the cup. Screaming, she slammed on the brakes as scalding hot coffee splashed all over her lap and stomach.

"Fuck!" she shrieked as the car began to skid in circles on the deserted road. "Oh shit," she wailed. The car finally came to an abrupt stop. When she looked up she was in the middle of the road, facing a WRONG WAY sign. The hair on her neck began to rise. This was a bad start to the night.

* * *

Teri slowly pulled out of the employee parking lot and headed west toward the highway. Her eyes began to fill with tears as she drove, though the blizzard conditions didn't stop her from pushing the truck past 65 mph. When she started to breathe erratically, she pulled over to the side of the road. She looked all around the truck cab and then outside through the windshield. She was disoriented and close to panic.

"Where the hell am I?" she screamed. She bowed her head and sat silent for several minutes. Her hands eventually stopped shaking. With her head still down, she put the pickup in drive and stepped on the gas. When she finally looked back up, she was going more than 65 mph again, her eyes were clear, and a slight grin crept across her face as she looked at and then passed the sign for Burbridge, or about the halfway point to Arkcliffe.

* * *

Claire was finishing her burger as she approached the employee parking lot and pulled up close to the security gates, buzzing herself through with her ID badge. She parked as close to the station as she could and got out of the car. Workbag in hand, she made her way across the tracks to pick up 442's equipment. She walked up the platform on track four to the engine as quickly as possible, but her legs were scalded through her jeans and her steps were short and tentative. She climbed up the side ladder, wincing with every rung, and entered the darkened engine cab.

Placing her work bag on the fireman's seat, she began to look through the engine's paperwork to make sure all the required tests had been performed and were up to date. Satisfied, she sat down in the engineer's seat and picked up the radio mic.

"Rescue engineer to the yardmaster, over."

"Yardmaster answering the rescue engineer. Claire, are you ready to depart?"

"Roger that," she answered. "So I'm flying solo and the conductor will be in place at Arkcliffe to make the move, and has the required paperwork, is that correct?"

"That's correct, Claire, the conductor is en route, probably almost there already. You're released to go, signal indication."

"Roger that," Claire acknowledged and began to release the brakes and pull the throttle out. "Rescue train departing St. Albans with a limited clear signal, CP 93, track four to track two, out." Claire set the mic back on the cradle and turned the wipers on. She noticed the snowfall had subsided considerably, and wished the painful burns on her stomach and thighs would do so too.

She looked over at her speed charts and began to notch the throttle out, approaching and then quickly passing 79 mph. "Okay, let's get this over with," she sighed and then leaned back in the seat as the train picked up speed. Within moments she was cruising at more than 90 mph. The snowfall appeared to increase with the speed of the train. Her view through the engine's windshield made it seem like she was being vacuumed up into some sort of space portal.

As she began to blow the horn for the upcoming crossing a mile in advance, the train's speed topped off at 110 mph.

* * *

Teri pulled off at the Burbridge exit and began to drive slowly through the small town south of the city. She spotted tire tracks cutting a path through the snow that led further into the woods and began to follow it, carefully maneuvering along the bumpy, ice-encrusted road.

* * *

Claire's neck had begun to itch and she knew her guides were trying to communicate with her. It was already hard enough to focus with the reduced visibility, and there was another crossing coming up. She attempted to block the intuitive part of her mind and focus on the road ahead of her. It didn't work: A picture of the WRONG WAY sign formed in her mind's eye. She shook her head trying to get rid of it, and began to blow the horn for the second crossing. She glanced at her watch. *Almost halfway there,* she thought with a sigh. *Focus, Claire.* She directed her gaze out the windshield through the snow at the tracks ahead.

* * *

Teri turned the truck's lights off as she pulled up to the small hunter's railroad crossing in the middle of the Burbridge woods. She pulled over behind a large pine and shut the engine off. Sitting still in the driver's seat, she sat looking expressionlessly toward the tracks ahead, then stepped out of the truck without a jacket, hat, or gloves, seemingly impervious to the sub-zero temperature. The wind whipped and howled in her face and slammed the truck door shut. She looked up and then began to walk toward the tracks, fifty feet away through the ice and snow.

* * *

As the train barreled along at 110 mph in the darkness, Claire grabbed a bottle of water from the engine's tiny floor fridge and took a long drink. When she looked up, she immediately threw the emergency brakes on. The train began sliding and squealing abruptly. She could see headlights at the upcoming hunters' crossing, illuminating a figure standing smack in the middle of the tracks.

"Oh my god! Oh my god! Oh my god!" she screamed as she closed in on the figure. The train slowed and then stopped only twenty feet from impact. Claire, who had closed her eyes tightly, opened them as the train stopped, only to see Teri, barely dressed and glaring angrily at the truck that had illuminated her presence on the tracks.

Her heart pounding, Claire called out an emergency transmission over the radio.

"Emergency, emergency, emergency," she began. "Rescue train in emergency at Burbridge center, over." Claire covered her face with trembling hands, looking down in shock at the cab floor as the dispatcher answered.

"Dispatcher calling the rescue train, what is the nature of the emergency, over?"

"There was a person on the tracks. We did not have impact, over."

"No one was hit, is that correct, rescue train?" the dispatcher asked.

"Roger," Claire confirmed. "It was a near miss."

"Is the trespasser still on the scene?"

Claire lifted her head and looked through the windshield onto the tracks. There stood two men in hunting gear, yelling as a truck spun around and began to drive away.

"FUCK!" Claire yelled, throwing the mic across the engine console.

The dispatcher's voice came back. "Dispatcher to the rescue train, is the trespasser still on the scene?"

Shaking her head, Claire picked the mic back up. "No," she replied, eyes tearing up. "They took off."

"Were they in a vehicle?"

"Yes, but I couldn't make it out."

"Are you okay to proceed to your destination?"

Claire sat for a long moment in silence. Brushing her hand across her forehead, she felt beads of sweat from the adrenaline coursing through her body. Seeing Teri on the tracks had her insides tied in knots, and a thousand terrified questions were clattering around in her head.

Taking a deep breath, she forced herself to sit up straight and push her shoulders back.

"Dispatcher to the rescue train, over."

"Rescue train answering," Claire replied softly.

"Okay to proceed from where you stand, dispatcher out."

"Copy that, okay to go from where we stand, rescue train out," Claire replied. Catching her breath, she released the brakes and then gently began to pull the throttle out. The adrenaline was still vibrating her nerves like guitar strings.

As she made her way to Arkcliffe, she realized two things. One, Teri was supposed to be her rescue conductor, and two, this might be the last time she would see her best friend alive. It was all sinking in now. Her eyes began to sting with tears as she rounded the final corner, approaching the broken-down train.

"Rescue train to the conductor, I am on the approach, over." Claire could see someone holding up a flare with a bright orange flame as she neared. Then a voice came over the radio, singing in a low, growling whisper: "He's got the whoooole world in his hands…he's got the whoooole world in his hands." A chill raced down Claire's spine as the light of the flare illuminated Teri's grinning face as she stood in front of the disabled train.

Claire stared down at Teri as she stopped the train directly in front of her. Her friend's eyes looked strange in the light of the flare, almost like someone else's. Her pupils appeared dark gray and glowed ominously.

Claire jumped out of the engineer's seat and pulled her jacket on. She yanked open the fireman's-side door and began to climb down the ladder.

"Listen, asshole!" she yelled before jumping off the bottom rung to the ground. She jerked her head up, but Teri was gone. Claire looked around. The two engines, standing face to face, roared as she looked into the woods through the darkness. She walked alongside the engine she was there to rescue and then back toward the coaches. Light shone through an open door, and she climbed up the trap stairs and onto the train.

The coach was filled with people, but half of them were sleeping. A few of the others glanced up at her, annoyed by their predicament. She walked through all four coaches and into the café car. There sat the two outlawed conductors, exhausted from being yelled at by the two hundred-plus passengers.

"Hey!" Lou, the lead conductor, called to her, his face immediately brightening.

"Rough night, huh?" Claire said, trying to muster a smile.

"Wasn't too bad," Lou said with a shrug. "The next person that calls me an asshole probably isn't going to like what happens next, though." He twirled one finger in a circle by his temple like he was losing it.

Claire looked around the car. "So where's your relief conductor?" she asked knowingly.

"Not with you?" Lou asked, frowning.

"No," Claire replied. "I thought they sent someone ahead of me."

"No one showed up yet, just you," he said, disappointed. "Great, we're never getting out of here."

Claire sat looking out the café car window into the darkness for a moment.

"Well, look, I'm the rescue engineer, but I'm also the road foreman. If you want, I can order you to work past your outlaw time and we can whip this mess back up to St Albans. Or I can call for another relief conductor and we can continue to wait...*asshole.*" She winked at him.

Lou laughed. "I'm in, let's do this," he said, standing up. "Let me get my coat and flashlight, and I'll be right behind you."

"Good deal," Claire gave a thumbs-up and headed back through the coaches. When she was back inside her engine, she called the dispatcher.

"Rescue train to the dispatcher, I have arrived at the disabled train, looking for permission to back up and then reverse direction to hook onto the equipment, over."

She sat waiting for the dispatcher to respond, her eyes throbbing from the stress.

* * *

Teri drove home, shoving Doritos into her mouth and staring angrily at the road. The weather had cleared up. She turned the radio on and leaned back in the seat, suddenly calm and softly singing along to Gary Wrights' "Dream Weaver." Her eyes became heavy and she began to close and then re-open them very slowly, and then finally she closed them for good and passed out as the truck continued traveling up the highway at more than 70 mph.

* * *

Feeling something touch her foot, Teri came awake with a jolt. Disoriented, she looked around her living room for a moment and then down at her feet. A bunch of sweatshirts and jeans were piled up next to the couch, and had fallen over on her. She opened and closed her eyes, yawning, and then looked over at the Ouija board box, which was sitting on the floor next to the table, unopened. Her eyelids became heavy as though she were being tugged away. Her eyes fluttered for a moment, and then closed as she passed out again.

CHAPTER 26

The Plot Thickens

"Hey, Don," Claire said to the outlawed engineer. "I just called Jim and told him that I am having you work over the hours of service so we can get this thing back up there and balance the equipment for tomorrow's trains. Why don't we do another quick briefing and a brake test? You are going to have to ride in your disabled unit in the middle and watch the gauges after I back onto you." She turned off her cell phone, preparing for the move.

"Yeah, sounds good. I sure don't want to wait another three or four hours to get out of here," Don said and began to climb down the side of Claire's engine to re-enter the disabled engine. "You think you'll take any heat when we pull in for ordering me, though?"

She shrugged her shoulders. "Rescue train calling the dispatcher, over," Claire spoke into the mouthpiece of the handset.

"Dispatcher answering, over."

"This is Road Foreman Montgomery. We have our paperwork and have completed all the necessary brake tests. Ready to make the back up move, when you can handle us, over."

* * *

About a half an hour later, the backup move complete, Claire communicated with the dispatcher a final time before finally heading back over the rails to St. Albans.

"Okay, rescue train with engine 1956, you have permission to depart Burbridge in advance of the signal on the main track, over."

"On the repeat, rescue train with engine 1956 has permission to depart Burbridge in advance of the signal, is that correct? Over."

"That is correct. Have a safe and good trip. Dispatcher out."

"Roger. Rescue train out."

"Conductor rescue train to the head end. I got that, okay to depart in advance of the signal. All buttoned up back here. Okay to highball. First restriction will be a thirty at milepost 116.9, over."

"Roger, departing Burbridge and a thirty ahead at milepost 116.9, out." Claire eased the throttle out to get the train moving and stretched out before adding a little more speed and doing a running brake test.

"Head end rescue train to the conductor, good on the running brake test, over," she said, using the foot pedal to key the mic.

"Roger, good on the runner," Lou replied.

"Head end to the conductor up to a clear in the cab. Here we go."

Claire's nerves were beginning to calm. The return trip was quiet. She marveled at the beauty of the star-filled sky, and at the fresh snow that glistened under the light of the nearly full moon.

Lost in the groove of the run and not having to worry about making station stops, she was relieved that the trip passed quickly.

The crackle of chatter on the radio let her know that she was about ten miles or so out of St. Albans, and that she would have to call the stationmaster when she crested the hill to see what the plan was going to be. She hoped that they had found a crew, and she really wanted to know what had happened to Teri. Suddenly a voice came over the radio.

"Station master calling the rescue train, over."

"Rescue train answering, over."

"Bringing you in on the Main. Once the passengers are clear, you and the utility conductor will bring it up to the goal post. Mechanical will be up there for the cut. Once you have it split, you need to report upstairs, over."

"Roger, discharge the passengers then up to the goal post for the cut. Report upstairs after the cut, out."

That is so strange, Claire thought, looking at her watch. It was almost 11:30 PM. *I wonder what's going on?*

She got all her paperwork together and re-packed her grip while the passengers exited the train. She had butterflies in her stomach, even though the run had gone well. Could she be in trouble for moving the train with an outlawed crew?

Maybe it's Teri who is in trouble for not showing up, and they want my side of the story. Guess I'll find out soon enough.

Another voice came over the radio. "Utility conductor to head end of the rescue train. We are clear back here; okay to pull it up to the goal post for the cut. I have us lined up, over."

"Roger, okay to pull up to the goal post. All lined up, out."

Moving the throttle to the second notch, Claire stood up and looked out the enormous windshield to make sure all the switches were lined up for them as they zigzagged over six tracks to reach the Archway track and the goal posts.

Stopping just a few feet shy of the posts, Claire reached over to the right to set the parking brake.

"Requesting three-point protection on the rescue train equipment, over."

Claire made sure the reverser was centered and put all the brakes on before knocking down the 480 head end power and placing the generator field switch in the off position. "Three point applied, over."

The radio broke Claire's thoughts. "Okay to release three point. Leave the 480 down, over."

She flipped the generator field switch up and continued to release the parking brake. "Three-point released and no 480, over."

"Utility conductor to rescue train, okay to pull ahead for the cut, over."

"Rescue train pulling ahead."

"Far enough."

That was it. Claire was done. Securing the equipment, she grabbed her grip and flung it over her shoulder, pulling her thick leather gloves on before opening the door.

The utility conductor, Jeff, was at the bottom of the stairs. "Hand your bag down," he offered.

"Thanks," Claire said, and slowly let the bag down to him by the straps.

"I've got the cart right here. I'll give you a ride to the station," Jeff said.

She thanked him and climbed into the front of the cart. Snow crunching beneath their wheels, they headed toward the station.

"Do you know who is still here? Any bosses?" Claire asked.

"There were a lot of them here earlier. The cops showed up when 464 pulled in."

"*What?*"

Jeff nodded. "They escorted Frank off the train and brought him upstairs in handcuffs. Rumors were flying like crazy. Some people said it was for stealing, and other people said it had to do with transporting minors. All I know is I have never seen that jerk without a smug look on his face until tonight. They wiped it right off of him," Jeff concluded with a shrug. He brought the cart to a stop by the crew room door.

"Thanks. I wonder what they want with me. Can hardly wait to find out." Claire jumped out of the cart and grabbed her bag.

"Good luck."

Opening the door, she saw that the hallway was deserted and the crew room was empty as well.

"Where is everyone?" she said aloud.

She climbed the stairs to the second floor. That was silent as well. Walking toward the yardmaster's office, she looked down the hall and noticed that all the other offices were dark and deserted.

"Hey, Craig, how are you? You wanted to see me?" Claire entered the relief station masters office with a quizzical look. Jim's shift had long since ended.

"Yeah, I just wanted to give you a heads-up that Frank was taken off the train tonight by the cops. I am not sure what is going on, but it has to do with underage girls. I heard bits and pieces, something about the trespasser strike a while back with that girl. There was a lot of yelling, too. Some cop was pretty jacked up, really ripping him a new one," Craig said.

"What do you mean the cop was jacked up?" Claire asked. "What was he saying? I know you know more than you are letting on," she pressed.

Craig shrugged innocently. Claire was losing her patience.

"Would you forget that I am management for five seconds? There is no way to save his reputation if the cops are involved. Besides, you know how the railroad works. If you don't tell me what's going on, I'll end up hearing some super-embellished version in a bar."

"All right," Craig conceded. "I heard them talking about some house on Springs Road."

Claire froze. "Springs Road?" she repeated, looking into his eyes. He squirmed.

"Yeah. The cop said he was going to bury him. He kept mentioning a house."

Claire swallowed hard, looked at the floor, and then looked back at Craig. "Are you sure he didn't say Milton Springs Road?"

"Yes!" Craig responded triumphantly. "Yes. Milton Springs Road."

Claire began to feel dizzy as Christine's words in the engine that night played back in her mind:

Wasn't the only one...He's here... She began to feel nauseated.

"Hey," Craig asked, worried. "You all right?"

Claire looked up at the ceiling and nodded.

"Frank looked like crap," he continued. "He was yelling: 'It was him! It wasn't me!' as the detective ushered him out."

"I'm done. I'm going to head home. Have a good night," Claire said.

* * *

"Milton Springs Road," she murmured to herself as she walked out into the cold night air. She wondered where Teri could be, and yet at this point she was almost afraid to find out. "This is nuts," she murmured, pulling her cell phone from her pocket. It was still powering up when she reached her car. She threw her grip in the back seat and got behind the wheel, turning the heat up full blast to defrost the windows and keep the blood flowing in her veins.

CHAPTER 27

UNFINISHED BUSINESS

Teri sat up on the couch in the darkness, staring straight ahead. There was a loud knock on her wall. Then another. Steady and loud they came, three in a row, single knocks spaced several seconds apart.

She rose from the couch and walked slowly through the living room to her bedroom without turning the lights on. Her path was illuminated in patches by the streetlights shining through the partially opened blinds.

She walked over to her dresser and grabbed a clean pair of jeans and a sweatshirt. She dressed emotionlessly and returned to the living room, where she picked up a claw hammer and her car keys from the end table. She walked out the door without closing it behind her.

Her lips were grayish, dry, and cracking. As she reached the driver's side of her car, she bent down and picked up a piece of dirt- and gravel-encrusted ice from the ground and put it in her mouth. She began to chew it as she opened the door. Her gums had already begun to bleed as she started the car. She set the hammer down on the seat beside her, turned the stereo up as loud as it would go, and put the car in drive.

* * *

Detective Bellissimo looked down at his watch: 12:30 AM. He sighed and stood up to stretch his legs. Walking around his desk, he yawned, picked up his coffee cup, and walked out to refill it from the machine.

He never saw Teri as she entered the station and stood silently, bent over the water fountain opposite the receiving desk, for several minutes. Finally, she stood up again and turned to face the desk, wiping her mouth with her arm. Bellissimo had his back to the glass as Teri slowly approached the window.

"Well, hello there, Detective." The low, scratchy female voice startled him and he spun around too quickly, spilling hot coffee down the front of his white dress shirt. Teri grinned at him from the other side of the bulletproof partition.

"Damn it!" he yelled, slapping at his chest, where the coffee was burning his skin. He glanced at her, then back at his shirt, becoming more uneasy each time he looked at her.

"What can I do for you, Ms. Cooper?" he asked, annoyed.

"I just wanted to thank you for helping me the other night," she began, still grinning.

"That's not a problem," he said, slowly regaining his composure. He grabbed a paper towel from his desk and looked at her again. "That probably could have waited until tomorrow," he added, mopping his chest.

She locked her eyes on his. "Well, I hear you are holding a friend of mine here, and I was hoping you would be kind enough to let me see him. Frank?"

He studied her face. It was so pale she looked like an albino. Her lips were gray and drowned-looking, and her eyes were completely bloodshot. They appeared to be filled with blood, and the red against her blue irises made her pupils seem gray. It was eerie.

"Is there anything you need to tell me?" he asked suspiciously. "Like I said to you and your friend, if there's a connection between you and these crimes, I'll find it, one way or another."

"We just work together," Teri countered. "Someone has to visit the guy."

Bellissimo could sense that Teri's feelings toward Frank were ultimately negative, despite her show of friendly concern. That reassured him. "Yeah, all right," he conceded. "Let me clean up here and I'll buzz you in." He walked into the men's room.

Teri waited, motionless, near the secured door.

"Okay," Bellissimo called out as he reappeared. "When you hear the buzz, go ahead and open it," he said, reaching under the counter.

There was a loud buzz and Teri pushed the door open, moving the hammer to the center of her back, under the waistband of her jeans.

"This way," Bellissimo said, motioning for her to follow him.

Teri began to follow and within seconds was right behind him. He turned around, startled.

"Wow," he said. "You're safe here, you know; you don't have to be on top of me."

Teri nodded silently and waited a few seconds, until the detective was a few feet ahead of her.

They turned a corner and headed down a long corridor lined with barred cell doors. He stopped about halfway down the hall in front of cell number 0013. Teri looked at the door number and then at the detective.

"Your 'friend' is in here," he said, disgusted. "Are you sure you want to talk to someone like this?"

"Boy, I sure do," she said, smiling eerily. Her voice dropping into a lower register.

Bellissimo pulled a large key ring from his belt. "It's none of my business, but you have shitty taste in friends."

Teri kept smiling, raised her eyebrows, and gave him a thumbs-up.

The detective shook his head and unlocked the triple-bolted cell door, slid it open, and stepped aside.

"You have a visitor, scumbag," he called into the cell as Teri slowly walked by him and toward Frank, who was sitting on a small mattress.

Bellissimo closed the door behind her and grabbed the bars on the outside as Frank looked up, confused. "Just call if you need me. He's not a danger to you, he only picks on children." He glared at Frank for a moment and walked away.

Teri turned her head slowly toward Frank. "Delivery boy," she sang softly, her voice lowering further still, becoming dark and masculine. Frank began to recoil.

"Teri?" he asked, disoriented. "Who—what are you doing here? What do you want?"

"You're what I want," Teri growled, stepping closer. Her pupils were now enormous and pale gray. Her teeth were beginning to darken, turning a deep yellow, almost orange.

"Get away from me!" he yelled. "What the hell is this?"

"Oh, that's perfect!" Teri said, laughing and clasping her hands together in pleasure.

Bellissimo was coming back down the hall toward the cell, his footsteps echoing on the concrete floor. Teri extended her hands toward Frank, her fingers curved like claws. "Boo!" she yelled in his face, stretching her fingers toward his neck.

"Help! Help me!" Frank shrieked. Terrified, he began pulling the end of the mattress up from its frame to cover his face, only to fall off the bed onto the floor.

"What's the problem, fruitcake?" Bellissimo said, peering into the cell.

Teri turned and looked at the detective. She smiled at him, but her lips were white and foaming. Her breathing had begun to sound like a dog's, low and rough.

Bellissimo stepped back.

"Hey, detective," Teri said, now speaking in the masculine voice of the entity, Doug. She pulled the hammer out of her waistband and held it up. "It's okay if I have this, right? Get 'em before he squeals on you too, detective?"

The entity began laughing hysterically. Shaking with fear, Frank curled into a tight ball and threw up on the floor.

Bellissimo ran down the hall and around the corner to his office. "What the fuck was that!" he yelled. "What the fuck *is* that!" He reached deep into his top desk drawer and pulled out the envelope marked Christmas Money. He shoved it in his pocket while looking frantically for his cell phone. He heard a thump—he'd knocked the phone onto the floor. He reached down and grabbed it with a shaking hand.

Down the hall, he heard the sound of bones breaking and meat being pulped. "Tasty Franky!" a hoarse, growling voice yelled, laughing. Frank began to scream as the hammer struck again and again.

Bellissimo hurriedly scrolled through his contacts until he found Claire Montgomery. He pressed send and waited, his hand clasping his chest.

* * *

"Good job, Franky boy," the entity sneered as Frank passed out from shock and pain in a pool of blood, vomit and urine on the cell floor.

CHAPTER 28

THE CROSSROADS

While she waited for her car to warm up and the windshield to clear, Claire's phone began buzzing with notifications she'd missed

She picked it up. There were nine new text messages and three missed calls with voice mails, all from Bellissimo. She shivered.

As she was about to return the call, the phone started buzzing. Bellissimo again. She answered immediately.

"What's going on that you're blowing up my phone, Detect—" Claire was cut off mid-sentence.

Bellissimo's voice was shaky with fear. "I got your friend Teri here and there is something seriously wrong with her. It's like it isn't her at all. She sounds like a man...and she is in the cell, tormenting this guy Frank. We're holding him here—he's in deep shit. I let her in the cell with him and then she started...changing. I locked her in there with him."

"You have Teri down there? She's with Frank? And what do you mean she's talking like a man?

And you locked her in a cell with him? What exactly is she doing?" Claire was almost as frantic as Bellissimo.

"She's just...talking in a really deep voice and acting like Frank is some long-lost buddy and she... doesn't look like herself. Just get down here," the detective pleaded.

"Listen," Claire began sternly. "She is possessed by that guy we hit with the train the other day. I know how that sounds, I know you don't believe me, but I don't give a shit right now. You just have to stay away from that cell. I'm on my way, and I'm going to call a couple of friends to join me. Whatever you do, don't let her out and don't get in there with her. *She will be able to take you down*," Claire warned, and hung up.

She put the car in gear and called Gia as she sped toward the police station.

"Hello?" The voice was sleepy and confused.

"Gia, it's Claire. The spirit has taken over Teri, she's at the police station. Detective Bellissimo— the asshole cop from the diner—has her locked in a cell with a guy who was arrested for something to do with underage girls. I think he and the entity Doug are connected. Please come to the station right away, and call anyone else you know to help," Claire pleaded.

Gia was wide awake. "I'll be there as soon as I can," she promised.

"Thank you. I don't know what I'm walking into," Claire stammered, picking at her scar.

"Be careful. Make sure you keep your shield up. Don't trust her no matter how she presents," Gia cautioned.

Claire mentally calculated the fastest route to North Main Street and the police station. Pulling up a few minutes later, she noticed several marked cruisers parked haphazardly along the front of the building. She leapt out of the car and ran up the front steps to the glass-enclosed area. She rang the bell and waited.

"Are you Claire?" came a frantic voice over a speaker.

"Yeah, I'm Claire." She looked up at a camera in a glass bubble and was buzzed in.

"We're down the hall," the voice on the speaker barked in a voice filled with tension.

She smelled rotten eggs mixed with blood. It was so strong, like a physical cloud, it nearly stopped her in her tracks. She pushed through.

Running down the hall, Claire saw three patrol officers standing outside a cell on the right, guns drawn. She couldn't see inside, but the officers' faces were grim and fearful. This wasn't good at all.

Reaching the cell, she looked in. Frank was curled up on the floor, clutching a badly broken arm to his chest. Bellissimo was suspended in midair, up against the wall. Teri was pacing back and forth in front of them, clutching a hammer. Her face was so contorted, she was almost unrecognizable.

"What took so long?" she growled at Claire. "You have no idea what's going on, do you?"

"I'm here now, Teri. Why don't you tell me," Claire said, struggling to keep her voice calm. Then she addressed Bellissimo. "How did you end up in there?" she scolded, seeing deep scratches on his face. She ran her hand down her scar. "I told you to wait for me."

"Aww. Isn't that the sweetest thing, Claire?" The entity laughed and snorted. "Now the two of you match!"

"She pretended she was being choked!" Bellisimo yelled incredulously. "I couldn't just let that happen." His words were interrupted by a maniacal laugh from Teri. "I barely got out an emergency call," he continued. "I came back to check on them and she ripped the radio out of my hand and locked me in here." He looked out at the three officers standing nervously in the hall.

"You know I'm not Teri," the entity said in a deep, growl. "You tried to get her into your stupid circle jerk so you could get rid of me. Guess what? Didn't work." Teri bared her teeth, which were stained with blood. Claire looked down at Frank. He had a large bite mark on his arm, just above the wrist.

"You want to try again?" the entity sneered.

Claire was staring directly into the face of evil. Some of the features might have been Teri's, but she was nothing more than a vehicle now.

"Smell something, Claire?" The entity asked. "Burning toast, is it?"

Claire froze and stared blankly. "What do you want with Teri? She can't do anything for you," she asked, trying to remain calm.

"It's not about her," the voice laughed. "I just needed a ride to make sure that Franky got what was coming to him."

The temperature in the room had dropped so low that Claire could see her breath, and the lights were flickering. Goosebumps covered every inch of Claire's body; the entity was sucking the energy out of the room. He was preying on those who had succumbed to their fear.

Teri's body looked down at Frank, weeping on the cell floor. "You always thought that you were so smart and that you could keep this hidden. Always putting on a show, being a good husband and pillar of the railroad. I knew smacking your little playmate with a train would shake you up. Don't look so surprised, Franky. You're just as bad as me and you know it."

Teri's face had now taken on the appearance of a deranged-looking older man. A dark cloud began wafting from Teri's body, seeming to leak from every pore, and it was drifting closer and closer to Frank.

"Doug?" Frank stammered in a panicked voice as he shrank away, trying to crawl under the bed.

"Of course it's me, you spineless piece of shit!" Doug yelled. Suddenly Bellissimo dropped to the floor, too; it looked to Claire like he twisted his ankle when he fell. "It was a fucking census taker, they don't count dead bodies. They never would have figured out where she went. You ruined everything," the deep, masculine voice said and then Teri spat in Frank's face. Saliva and blood trickled down his cheek.

The dark mist reentered Teri's body, which twitched like it was gaining strength. Pivoting and glaring at Bellissimo, the entity growled, "That little knife your Daddy gave you isn't going to help you, fucker, so don't even try."

Bellissimo had been clutching the pocketknife; he let it fall out of his hand to the cell floor.

Locking eyes with the detective, Claire spoke. "What did Frank ruin?" she asked.

Teri's body turned, and her face contorted around a thin-lipped smile like a jackal. It grunted as it glanced, steely-eyed, at Claire, who kept her focus on the detective to remain calm.

"We had the perfect setup. Frank and me, we liked 'em young. So did our customers. We bought 'em for a few hundred dollars and smuggled them in. We'd pick from dozens of 'em, from all over the world. Like a never-ending parade of tasty treats. Franky had a gift, too; he always picked the best meat. They'd come in on cargo ships, and then he'd transport them to me on the trains."

Glancing at Frank, the entity snarled, "He used to brag about testing them out. Didn't you, delivery boy? It was a win-win. Money and pussy for both of us, and he fucked it up," the guttural-toned voice from Teri's mouth went on. "Christine was his special little girl—his favorite. But he panicked after he accidentally killed her. I stored her in my freezer, keeping both of us safe. But then Franky boy dropped the dime on me, so I put her ass on the train tracks to get his attention."

The cell grew quiet. The entity inched closer to Claire, tilting its head from side to side like a snake as he approached with a crazy, almost child-like grin.

"Someone in here with us likes you a *lot*, Claire." The entity tipped its head all the way back, laughing. "Got a message from your mom, too. Says burnt toast is good for you!"

Claire closed her eyes tightly and looked down at the floor. She could feel hot tears forming.

"Thaaaaaaat's right," the entity hissed. "You remember. How sweet. Too bad mommy's not here to help your ass now."

Suddenly Claire felt a warm feeling, like hands on her shoulders. Her eyes widened and she looked back up at the creature. She glanced at Bellisimo, then Frank, then the officers in the hallway. Finally, she returned her gaze to Teri.

"That's great," she said matter-of-factly. "But you haven't finished telling me about Frank."

The entity's expression went blank for a moment, looking at Frank with eyes that now seemed to have two sets of pupils—the larger gray set hovering just above Teri's small black ones.

"I liked them young," it said, with a small grin that slowly became an ear-to-ear smile. The entity was drooling and rubbing its hands together. "I wanted new talent. He wouldn't help. Said he was out of the business. I tried to use local girls, but they were bland. No exotic treats." The creature smacked its lips and stuck out its tongue, licking its fingers and releasing a low groan.

Teri was completely inhabited by the entity Doug. When she spoke, the foul stench Claire knew so well enveloped the entire room. The heaviness of the air was almost unbearable.

"I would occasionally find a sweet little morsel, but it wasn't enough," Doug went on. "Franky used to bring over Girl Scouts in his van, with their delicious little cookies. It was too much. I really wanted one of those delicious little fuckers. I couldn't help it. And Frank? Do the math: He brought them to me, so there's only one person that could have dropped the dime." He looked over at Frank. The stench in the room had grown so thick that Claire, Frank, and Bellissimo all began to gag.

It's not burnt toast, Claire thought. *Burnt hair and sulfur. Burnt hair and sulfur.*

Again, drool was showing at the corners of Teri's mouth as the entity reached one hand toward her crotch. Realizing that what he was reaching for wasn't there, he became agitated.

"I know why I got caught," he growled. "But I'm not going anywhere until he gets what's coming to him."

Claire knew there was no reasoning with the creature. She had to get him crossed over against his own will—to banish him from this plane of reality. But it was going to be extraordinarily difficult to raise the vibration in the room, with all the negativity and fear gripping everyone.

Just then, the buzzer sounded and one of the young officers rushed to see who it was. A few seconds later, five women were headed down the hall. All of them were wearing some sort of sleepwear under their winter coats. Claire didn't recognize any of them, but she was grateful that they had come and knew that Lola and Gia must be close behind.

As the women approached the cell door, Claire said, "I need to raise the vibration. Can you guys send light and love into the cell?"

The entity began to size the women up. "You're all going to burn!" it snarled through Teri.

"He's looking for weakness," Claire said, raising her voice above his. "Don't engage."

"Wait, Claire!" the entity interjected sarcastically. "I don't exist, remember?" He laughed heartily, slapping Teri's knees. The women looked at Claire, confused.

"Officers," Claire said, "you need to step back and give us some room to work. No matter what you see or hear, do not interfere. We will get everyone out of there, including this piece of shit, with no one getting hurt. Just give us some room."

Gia and a very sleepy-looking Lola both arrived moments later, dressed in bathrobes and slippers and carrying besoms (brooms made of twigs, tied around a stick) and candles. The seven women proceeded to sweep in a circular motion around the cell.

One more pajama-clad woman arrived behind Gia and Lola; she, too, carried a candle and besom.

A total of eight women stood in a circle. Each of them lit her candle.

Doug laughed, blowing the candles out with such force that the officers in the hallway lost their hats.

The women looked at Claire. She nodded and they lit the candles again. The entity laughed harder as he blew them out again.

Claire took a deep breath and looked back at the cell door. Thea had shown up as well, standing just outside of the entrance, carrying a very large, very old Book of Shadows.

"Hey!" the entity hissed. "Is that your leader?" Teri clasped her hands together as the entity laughed so hard he began to cough.

Thea ignored his presence and walked calmly to Claire while slowly turning the tea-stained pages written in the witches' alphabet. She was completely unaffected, as if she were doing nothing more than carrying a blueprint through a construction site.

The ancient book was alive with drawings of the planets and adorned with pictures of gems that worked with the spells contained in its pages. There were also flowers and other plants pressed between the leaves that correlated with the spells' ingredients.

Thea stopped on a page toward the back of the book. It featured a drawing of nine brooms laid bristle to handle, crossing each other and forming a perfect circle.

Thea touched Claire's shoulder and pointed down at the page. Scribbled in the top left-hand corner was the word "toast." Claire jerked her head up and looked at Thea in bewilderment. The older woman winked at her.

"How did you—" Claire began, but Thea cut her off.

"Read it, Claire," she ordered calmly. "You will recognize the words. You will know what you have to do."

As Thea and Claire stared at one another, the other women grabbed their besoms and formed most of the circle as shown in the spell, leaving space for one broom.

Thea, breaking eye contact with Claire, looked around the cell for a moment. Ignoring the entity they had now surrounded, she glanced at one of the officers standing outside.

"Open the door," Thea commanded neutrally. Her eyes seemed to blaze with inner light. She motioned to Bellissimo and Frank to enter the circle near the entity, Doug. The two men reluctantly did so and Claire, who was still in a trancelike state, laid down the last of the besoms, completing the circle.

Thea handed her the Book of Shadows. It was the biggest and heaviest Claire had ever seen. She clutched it tightly.

Claire's physical body was present, but she was no longer with them. In her mind's eye, it was thirty years earlier, and she was trying to scream. The clawed hand dug into her face and throat as her mom charged into the room. The words that she had spoken had been Latin. Claire began to replay them in her mind, to mutter the words as she had heard them. Soon they were changing. As she muttered the words over and then over again, they slowly became part Latin and part English, and then half Latin and half English.

The women stopped what they were doing, watching and listening as Claire's indecipherable mutterings became full English sentences. Suddenly, she fell silent. Her green eyes grew larger and she glared at the entity.

Thea nodded and motioned to the women, who began to form two shapes outside the broom circle. The first shape was composed of five women stationed at the points where a pentacle would be, representing the human form. Two legs, two arms, and a head, with each point representing one of the elements and aspects of a person: earth, air, fire, water, and the spiritual.

The second shape was made up of four women, who assembled themselves into a circle representing the four elements alone, as an extra shield to keep them protected. Once in place, the women in the outer circle began to light their candles again, and this time they stayed lit.

The entity had begun to look disoriented, and Thea quickly began to recite one of the ancient chants from the book as the power of the circle grew stronger.

The women in the inner pentacle were now able to successfully light their candles as the entity began losing power. One woman lit a piece of Palo Santo incense and fanned it toward the middle as the smoke drifted upward. Another woman, dressed in a dark green robe, opened her canvas bag and started cautiously throwing cedar chips around the cell to contain the evil.

"Here, replace all the bulbs you can with these red ones," said an elderly lady dressed in footy pajamas, as she handed out lightbulbs to the others. "It will be easier for us to see what is going on." Even though he was becoming disoriented, the entity still had power, and the women quickly changed the three bulbs in the cell, replacing them with the red ones.

Working in unison, the women gathered back together and began chanting: "Oooo...Aaaa... Eeee...Oooo...Aaaa...Eeee..." until it became one fluent sound.

"I got a better one," the entity laughed, though it sounded slightly winded. "Let's do something from the Stones!"

The officers and all of the women fell silent and stared at Claire, who stood glaring at the entity. Finally, Lola resumed the chant and the others followed. Soon, the sound of a baritone voice from one of the officers could be heard, followed by another, until they were all chanting. The feeling in the room seemed to lighten, but *Is it enough?*, Claire thought to herself.

Motioning to the others to keep singing, she silently cast another circle around the entire group. She made the perimeter high and strong to protect those outside of the cell—and more importantly, Teri's body and Bellissimo inside the innermost circle.

Claire closed her eyes and took a deep breath. She visually transported herself back to the class she had taken on crossing over stubborn spirits and those that were confused and didn't know the way. This was different, though.

Claire had only ever dealt with spirits that wanted to pass messages to their loved ones. She had heard about haunted houses and malevolent spirits, but this entity wasn't confined to a house or a doll. This was an earthbound evil spirit, and it was inside her best friend. She knew the cost that might be exacted to get rid of it. She had dealt with that every day of her life. The loss of her mother had left a forever-gaping hole in her heart—and the scar. The awful scar.

Pulling her wits together, she called in the Archangels to assist from the other side. Calling on Angels was something Claire had never done before. She remembered her teacher telling her that anytime you needed serious help, it was okay to call in the big guns. *Well, here goes,* she said to herself as she threw her shoulders back and braced herself to battle Doug one on one.

"Ladies, I have cast a circle, so we are safe on this side of the cell. I need you all to hold hands and keep the circle from being compromised, and to keep chanting," Claire ordered.

"Guys, put your guns down, they aren't going to help us now," she told the policemen. "Step behind the ladies and help them chant. Don't let it feel your fear. He will use it against you. Focus," she commanded.

Walking to the wall, Claire bent down and began making small cutting motions with her hand from the floor up, making sure to move the cedar chips out of the way as she worked. Standing upright, she stretched her hands above her head and continued cutting, standing on her toes to reach as high as she could. She continued cutting horizontally for a few feet before working her way down the wall with her hands.

As she worked, Claire chanted, "This is a one-way door. You can come to the bottom of the stairs and wait, but you cannot cross back to this side. This is a one-way door..."

Once she had reached the floor again, she turned to look at the officers, whose pale faces showed disbelief at what they were seeing.

"You can stop chanting. I have the doorway cut open," she said. Turning her attention back to the wall, she started calling out as if she were beckoning someone upstairs to come to down for dinner.

"I ask that anyone connected to this spirit come and help bring him back to the divine source."

"Doug," Claire called out to the entity.

Teri's body turned toward her, eyes glaring. "What?"

"I want you not to be afraid. You may have done things here, but you don't need to be afraid to go toward the light." Claire made her voice as soothing as she could.

"Go fuck yourself," the entity snarled back.

"It is all love. You can go now and you will be taken care of," Claire said softly.

"What the fuck are you talking about?" the entity snapped.

Claire watched and waited. Normally the portal would produce a glowing light. But it wasn't something that had to happen. This time it hadn't for some reason.

"Mom, is that you?" Doug asked, his voice losing some of the sharpness that it had had previously. The pale gray circles that had replaced Teri's pupils were beginning to darken.

The chanting had stopped. Everyone stared at Doug in silence.

"I'm afraid, Mom," Doug said, his voice taking on the timbre of a young child. Teri's head tilted to one side as the entity listened to something inaudible to the rest of them.

"Will I be in trouble?" he asked in that same childlike whisper. He was quiet, looking into nothingness. "Are you sure?" he asked again.

"I don't want to review my life! I don't want to learn any more lessons," Doug blurted. Teri's body recoiled and plastered itself against the wall, like a child that didn't want to eat its broccoli.

Foam was forming around Teri's mouth and her body twitched and contorted, flinging itself around the small cell. The voice that was coming out of Teri's mouth was slightly softer, but still masculine, and just as vile as it had been earlier. Everyone in the room knew that they were witnessing a conversation from the other side.

There was a long silence. Doug, the entity, was weeping now and nodding slightly.

"Is that you, Aunt Betty? Is that you too, Gram?" The voice seemed to be gaining hope.

All eyes were on Teri as the hammer the entity had been holding fell from her hands and hit the ground with a loud *crack*, chipping a piece of the concrete floor and sending it flying. Tears streamed down her cheeks. Her defensive stance was giving way to a swaying motion, and then her body slid down the wall and came to rest on the floor.

Claire sighed with relief and walked over, stopping just before Teri's limp body.

A gray mist manifested out of Teri and wrapped around Claire's head like a tentacle, pushing her forcefully down to the floor. Claire's head jerked back and forth as if she was being punched over and over again, and blood burst from her nose. The mist withdrew back into Teri's body and the entity jumped up and began to howl. It stood over

Claire's body as though daring anyone to take a step forward.

Claire began to recover. The entity looked down at her and grabbed her by her scarred face with one clawed hand, laughing evilly and lifting her off the floor.

"Remember this, little one?" he sneered, digging into the scar. She began to gush blood.

Without a word, Thea cracked him on the back of the head with the heavy book, and Claire fell to the floor. All of the women rushed to her aid, but Thea raised her hand to stop them.

"This belongs to Claire," Thea said. "Stay back. It will be what it must be."

A small, bright orb came through the portal Claire had cut and came to rest over her shoulder. Soon there was another. The women gasped and gazed, mesmerized. One of the officers passed out on the floor with a thud. Lola raced over to check him.

Claire slowly rose to her feet whispering in a chant that became louder and faster as she stood up from the floor. A fearful look spread over the entity's face as it began to comprehend Claire's words. He began to convulse as Claire leaned over him, her large green eyes seeming to stab him over and then over again as she spoke.

Her blood was pouring out of the reopened gash on her neck and face but she continued to chant over him, unfazed:

"The powers the power of three times three, to whence you return, so mote it be. The powers the power of three times three, to dust you return, so mote it be. The powers the power of three times three, to dust and to whence you came, so mote it be. The powers the power of three times three, Ancient Ones take him, so mote it be."

The entity began to lift slowly off of the floor. His twisted features faded back into Teri's softer ones. Claire's heart raced, and her eyes filled with tears as she watched her best friend's limp, exhausted body rise into the air.

A warm orange glow materialized from the portal as Teri floated toward the opening. Her body hung suspended in midair at the opening. Suddenly a putrid, dark gray mist extruded from her like a cloud of squid's ink, and was sucked into the portal with a blood-curdling scream.

The warm orange glow began to dissipate and Teri's body slowly sank to the floor as though guided by invisible, gentle hands. Soon the brightness had completely vanished into the invisible portal in the wall, as though it had never existed. Seconds later, only the dim light of the red bulbs and the cool light of the fluorescent tubes on the ceiling lit the cell.

"Open the cell door," Claire called to the officers, as Gia tended to her wounds. Everyone in the room was trembling. "Lola, can you check on Teri?"

Turning back to the wall, Claire started solemnly working as if she were using drywall and plaster to repair the portal she had opened. It took several minutes. As she worked, the women all lowered their hands in front of them and moved them back and forth, to disconnect from the energy field that had been created.

Bending down, they worked together to scoop up the cedar chips. The large piece of Palo Santo was extinguished, but the smoke and aroma still filled the cell.

The disbelief in the room was almost tangible. No one, not even the witches, were quite sure what had just taken place.

Suddenly, Claire heard Teri's voice. Just Teri's voice. Her heart skipped a beat.

"Where the hell am I? Why are you all staring at me and what the fuck is that smell?" Teri said, holding her hand on her head.

"You don't know?" Bellissimo asked, clearly shaken.

"Why the hell am I here, and who puked on the floor? Ugh, is that piss? Gross, there's blood all over the place, too!" She stared at Claire impatiently. "Are you gonna tell me what's going on, or what?"

"You really don't know?" Bellissimo repeated.

"Of course she doesn't know," Lola said, rolling her eyes.

The oldest of the officers opened the cell while the other two grabbed Frank and pushed him toward the wall. Turning him around, they cuffed him and led him away from the cell to get medical attention. As they left, one of the officers told him, "None of this shit happened, and you keep your fucking mouth shut."

Each of the women gave Claire a hug as they headed down the hall to leave. Lola and Gia stayed behind.

"You will always have a place with us," Gia said. "You never have to feel alone."

"That's right. You fit right in here," Lola said and turned back, looking briefly at the tall, brown-eyed detective. "Not bad," she said, tapping Gia on the shoulder.

Gia shook her head as they walked toward the receiving desk to leave the building.

Thea stood staring at Claire with a gleam in her eyes. "You don't need to label it any longer, Claire. You know now."

Claire's eyes teared up and she wrapped Thea in a rib-cracking embrace. "Thank you so much, Thea. I don't know how you knew but..." Thea cut her off.

"You know who sent me. She also wants me to remind you to always trust your nose." Thea winked and walked out of the cell. Claire bore a faint, appreciative smile as she watched her leave.

Bellissimo nodded at the remaining officers, who followed the women, escorting them out to their vehicles.

Claire sat down next to Teri on the cell's small mattress. "I feel hung over," Teri said softly.

Claire put her arm around her friend's shoulders as Bellissimo waved from the doorway to get Claire's attention. He told her he would be right back.

Claire nodded at him briefly as she pushed Teri's hair back behind her ears.

Bellissimo returned with a glass of water and two aspirin. Claire looked up and held her hand out. He placed the small pills in her hand, his gaze lingering, and waited as Claire took the glass of water. Nudging Teri, she gently handed her the aspirin.

Still a little disoriented, Teri swallowed the aspirin and then took a small sip of water.

"Why are we in a jail cell?" Teri asked.

"Well, our detective friend here said this was going to be where we're heading, so he decided to show us and scare us straight," Claire answered, looking up and giving Bellissimo a wink.

He chuckled uneasily, then turned and walked away, down the long hallway.

Claire smirked watching him leave, and stood up from the mattress. "C'mon, Teri," she said, holding out her hand. "Let's get out of here."

Teri let her friend pull her to her feet. "I had the strangest dream," she said, furrowing her brow as Claire helped her down the hallway.

"And what was that?" Claire asked, relieved but exhausted. They passed through the secure doors and left the police station.

"I was standing in this big field at night, and the grass was like four feet tall, and I was trying to find you."

"Did you?" Claire asked, laughing, as she opened her car door.

"Kinda," Teri said, sliding into the passenger seat.

As Claire walked around the car to the driver's side, she saw Bellissimo standing in the police station doorway, looking at her. She stared at him for a moment, then got in the car.

"Everywhere I looked, your head and then my mother's head would peek up from behind the grass, but it was like whack-a-mole," Teri continued. "Every time I would get to where I thought you were, a black clown's head with horns would pop up."

"So you didn't get to me?" Claire asked with a grin.

Teri shrugged. "I must have, because the last time I was moving in the field toward you, I woke up and there you were."

"That's one weird dream," Claire said as she backed out of her parking space.

"Hey, where are my smokes?" Teri asked, rooting around in the console.

Claire rolled her eyes. "You don't need to smoke every five minutes, do you?"

"Oh, stop it," Teri said. She found a cigarette in her pocket, lit it, and blew smoke out the window.

Rubbing her head, and still wondering what had happened, Teri tried to put things together, but many of the details were missing.

CHAPTER 29

CLEAN SWEEP

On the drive over to pick up Teri, Claire looked up at the brilliant blue sky and was amazed by the vast expanse that she knew existed between where she was now and where she would some- day be. The thought was humbling as well as exhilarating.

When she arrived at Teri's house, she jumped out of her car, feeling happier than she had since before this whole thing started. Walking up the driveway, she barely knocked before entering.

Looking around, she was stunned. For the first time since she had known Teri, the couch wasn't cluttered with clothes. In all the years that she had been coming over, she had no idea that there were designs on the armrests. It was the first time that she could actually see the whole room.

"What's gotten into you?" Claire giggled, en- tering the kitchen.

"I don't know, I just thought it was time for a change," Teri said as she rinsed the last of the dishes that were normally just stacked in the sink.

"Come on, we'll be late for our pedicures. You know how I love them." Claire grinned as she grabbed Teri's coat from the rack for her.

There was a lot Teri still wanted to know about the events at the police station. She had been bringing it up here and there, but wasn't really prepared to hear it all yet.

Claire didn't push, and didn't volunteer information. When Teri was truly ready, they would sit down and talk it all through from beginning to end, in full detail. Right now, they needed a nice, relaxing afternoon off.

Teri's sarcastic voice pulled her back to the here and now. "Yes, I know you love them. This time it's your treat. You owe me." She was joking, but there was some seriousness mixed in.

Walking from the house to the car, Teri pointed at the remnants of the snow angels, whose outlines had almost completely disappeared beneath fresh white snow from the night before. Claire heard a sigh escape from her friend's lips, followed by the barely audible word *bullshit*, before they both eased into the car.

"That's my girl," Claire said with a chuckle as they drove up the mountain toward the salon.

Just as she turned on the car radio, Claire's cell rang. Pulling it from her pocket, she glanced at the screen. Restricted. She knew who it was. "Hello, Detective," she said.

"Hi, Claire," the detective said and then hesitated. "I was just wondering if you might be interested in helping me with something? I was thinking maybe we could go to dinner and discuss it."

"Discuss what?" Claire asked, looking over at Teri and shrugging as she mouthed the word *Bellissimo.*

"We're having some problems with a missing person case, and I was thinking that maybe you might be able to hel—"

Claire ended the call and threw her phone onto the back seat.

"You don't want to help the nice detective?" Teri asked with a grin, taking a drag of her cigarette and flicking her ashes out the window.

"Help him?" Claire asked. "I have a brand new bottle of cayenne *just* for him."

The two women laughed.

"I'll call him later. Maybe."

A moment later, the Atlanta Rhythm Section came over the radio and they began to sing along: "Love is kinda crazy with a spooky little girl like you..."

Claire turned the volume up and they leaned back in their seats and laughed as they continued toward town.

CPSIA information can be obtained
at www.ICGtesting.com
Printed in the USA
BVHW04s0350050518
515205BV00001B/39/P